# THE GAME ENTREPRENEUR

# THE
# GAME
# ENTREPRENEUR

## GEORGE KONSTAND

**BALBOA.**
PRESS

A DIVISION OF HAY HOUSE

Balboa Press books may be ordered through
booksellers or by contacting:

Balboa Press
A Division of Hay House
1663 Liberty Drive
Bloomington, IN 47403
www.balboapress.com.au
1 (877) 407-4847

Printed in the United States of America.

ISBN: 978-1-4525-2447-4 (sc)
ISBN: 978-1-4525-2448-1 (e)

Balboa Press rev. date: 06/24/2014

# CONTENTS

# INSPIRATION

French cultural theorist Michel de Certeau gives his account[1] of Michel Foucault's response at a press conference in Belo Horizonte in Brazil in his introduction to *The Archaeology of Knowledge*:

> What, do you imagine that I would take so much trouble and so much pleasure in writing, do you think that I would keep so persistently to my task, if I were not preparing ... a labyrinth ... in which I could lose myself ... Do not ask who I am and do not ask me to remain the same: leave it to our bureaucrats and our police to see that our papers are in order. At least spare us their morality when we write (1972, 17).

# PREFACE

For the purpose of this book and in the context of the entrepreneur, "winning the game" refers to creating a valuable brand that is both influential and productive for the greater purpose of achieving a level of financial freedom.

*The Game Entrepreneur* is built on one key strategy: to understand humanity through a series of insights, revealing the nature of human behavioural and motivational tendencies. Insights reveal themselves in order of relevance, mimicking levels of consciousness within the brain. Understanding relevance is an opportunity to influence. Influence is value. Value is wealth. The conversion of human insights into material wealth is a matter of branding. Our ability to comprehend the relationship between the real and the imagined provides a space for doing good business. Entrepreneurs must seek to understand the world as though it exists in the realm of mythology as opposed to a sacred and unquestionable series of truths.

The game theory depicts the perceptual havoc that entrepreneurialism plays on the mind, the incessant questioning of everything we see and the realization that reality is something we imagine, attributing truth to experience, in a process of nurture.

As entrepreneurs trying, failing, and succeeding is always more about learning than anything else; therefore, winning is the measure of knowledge. A dramatic irony comes with learning, and that involves having to unlearn things first. Knowledge is not what we know. It is an awareness of the things we've learnt, relative to time and space, that we imagine to be real and true.

Realness and the truth seemingly juxtapose reality, and at some point, the entrepreneurial mind becomes riddled with suspicion that it is being played by something no more or less precise than it.

The game is realizing life in question. It is the knowledge that we choose to play or be played in a game that, in fact, has been prescribed to us as a reality. Winning is a matter of entrepreneurial perspective.

For as long as we reside on planet Earth, we are in the business of selling to human beings. This is a book about business. It's a how-to market book. It's a write-up on branding and how to build a brand, generate value around that brand, and exchange that value for money.

*The Game Entrepreneur* conveys underlying ideals of higher consciousness that require we give nature the same opportunity we have given to nurture in the hope that the future gives birth to a conscious entrepreneur. These underlying ideals are somewhat utopian, but should we not afford utopian ideals the same opportunity that we have granted capitalist ones?

Innovation is a possibility only made real through question. Question everything.

# LETTER FROM THE AUTHOR

Dear Entrepreneur,

I always envisioned that this book would someday come to life, but I hardly expected that it would be the catalyst for so much change in my world so soon. This book has absolutely consumed three years of my life. The process of now summing up my ideas and releasing them to the world is a numbing feeling, but not in a bad way. It's more like a Frank Ocean "Novacane" kind of numb, where the feelings are cool and euphoric but the process of losing control is an uncomfortable one.

For me, the idea of an entrepreneur is someone who is compelled to seek and create change. I have learnt that ideas inspire more enthusiasm in humans than money and that we can engage our innate super-humanness by harnessing creative energy. There is nothing like an entrepreneur with an idea. We wrestle with nature and nurture for the opportunity to create something and to see it grow. We have an appetite for the unknown, and for that, we seek out those who'll meet us, like-mindedly, in its unfamiliar.

I started writing *The Game Entrepreneur* back in 2011 when my initial name for the book was *The Game Young Entrepreneur.* I quickly became uneasy with the notion of a *young entrepreneur* because of how definitively the world associated youth with age. Time, like age, is just another construct put there to make us feel a certain way about ourselves. Entrepreneurs must realise that age is insignificant and youth is a matter of the heart. Children ask questions, play, and imagine. And so I'd liken any entrepreneur, regardless of age, to the brand of youth. But for the sake of keeping things simple, I dropped "young" from the title.

Looking back at the three years that passed, the memories are platonic; I have no real recollection of time passing. The book changed me in a way that I was unable to invest in the world emotionally and so, to the process of writing and questioning, I'd attribute only the sentiment of being calm, something of great clarity.

To write this book with purpose and intention required me to detach my ego and, in turn, place you, the reader, at the centre of my mind. What the hell would be the purpose of writing a book where all I did was talk about my experiences and feelings without at least theorizing about the parts that actually came together to form good business?

I must say I have not experienced anything quite like having to write a book. I have never loved and hated something so much at the same time. I have never wanted to quit something so much in my life. It took me four versions of this book, countless attempts at finding my voice and (possibly) border-lining on bipolar disorder, before settling on just one personality that I was content with, never ecstatic about but satisfied with. Sometimes it's better that we, entrepreneurs, stop thinking about things and just do them.

Often, our hesitation to just do comes from a sense of unrelenting fear that stops us from becoming the people we want to become. It's like fear and distraction came together to create a love child, procrastination. Procrastination is spoiled for choice, hungry for attention, and always seems to have an appetite for food and Instagram. I remember mornings when I would wake up, dress in a suit, and catch the peak-hour train into TownHall. I'd sit at a café, watch the people rush by sipping on a weak long black coffee (no matter the anxiety, coffee remained a staple). Then I would casually go back home.

I craved that feeling of normality. Nobody rewards abnormality, and so the feeling of failure is something that's always present. I often had to remind myself that I chose this path. That peak-hour train ride was how I reminded myself of the things I didn't want and it reinforced the need to choose the things I did want.

*The Game Entrepreneur* became something of a necessity for me, and only now I think about how entitled choice can make us and how one entitled entrepreneur can create something out of nothing because we see its necessity.

My break-up with normality left me reeling at the notion of modern humans in a civilised world. The thing with trying to understand reason is that it can only be understood after it has been reasoned with in question. To question requires having to seek out debate in real life in the third dimension with no filter. Coming to learn stuff takes time; coming to unlearn stuff takes an emotional breakdown, a rejection of everything you know, an exorcism of just about everything you believe, and twenty damn kilos, apparently, which for an ex-high school fat boy, is the most frustrating of all ... It's not surprising to me now, why the majority of the world chooses not to question anything.

For a brief time, it felt like I had lost my mind, but as with the blur of time passing, it seems mindfulness replaced the mindless banter that rendered *thinking* counter productive. The ability to exist without the need to defend what I knew, gave life to innovation as I sought to understand the things I didn't know.

I've learnt to accept the waves—the waves of failure and success and the waves of inspiration and depression—because waves are normal and natural. Waves represent the ocean, the weather, sound, light, smell, energy, and time. Everything else—stability, security, and perfection—is in fact abnormal. This leads to the question: Why then are we taught to seek what is abnormal? What a dysfunctional way of being! This explains why we are motivated to seek happiness in the most unloving people and to allow being enslaved in labour we hate, calling the most dysfunctional situations normal in the name of stability, security, and perfection.

This book is no fairy tale. Fairy tales are dysfunctional because they are perfect. Fairy tales are what we use to sell to dysfunctional people seeking perfection. This is marketing! I would describe this book as the simplest complex book ever written. The difference between its simplicity and its complexity is really a matter of entrepreneurial perspective: how objective we remain about objects. I often refer to the movie *Fight Club* (1999). I think I watched it fifteen times over the last three years. "The things you used to own, now they own you." I theorise about the world and the things we have come to own. And in saying that, my advice to all who read this book is exactly what I tell the people I love when giving them advice. "Take the words from my mouth, remove me and my delivery from the equation, apply those words to your life, and you will see change (for the better)."

I am a twenty-seven-year-old entrepreneur, born and raised just west of the golden city of Sydney, Australia. I belong to the type of income family that taught me money didn't grow on trees and the only way to get ahead in the world was to pick up a book and read the damn thing. I'd describe my parents as logical, they cared more about the institution of family than they did any religion or politic – they punished themselves with backbreaking work, figuring it's what they deserved for not reading more books. Books were respected in my household, along with backhanders for children who were out of line. I respected that. That line became the measure of all things for me. It taught me binaries—good and evil, wrong and right, and all the institutions that upheld these binaries—to some degree I think my parents would have preferred it if I just accepted these binaries as truth and not continued to stubbornly ask, "Why? Why are they true? Who created them? When? And who were they? What makes them any better than you or I? Said who?"

Consider that, in order for something to be true or for us to believe in it, we have to want to. The question is never about what or who but always about why. Now, this statement is hardly groundbreaking. But what is curious to me is the very little we seem to want to know about *why*. This is where it gets interesting. What if we could possess a perspective that allowed us to play with why, influence why, shape why, and change why. Then it all becomes a game of influence.

I have gathered that *why* is something we manifest from our ego. Deconstructing the ego is a matter of perspective. The game theory is based on the ancient Delphic teaching of "Know Thyself."

Everything I had ever studied from marketing to humanities, sociology, and even acting led me to this one teaching, so I decided to pursue it, all the way back to Delphi, Greece. It seemed inevitable that my research would lead me to Greece, so I set upon a six-month research project into "Know Thyself."

It was 2012, and Greece was also at the centre of an economic meltdown. I still question if the timing that it all happened was something of a coincidence or something more. It seemed ironic to me that I found myself creating opportunities in a country bankrupt of all of them. It became apparent to me that nowhere else in the world was there a body of people more uplifted and equally stifled by their ego than the Greeks. They became the perfect subjects for my research. After all, they pride themselves on the work of the greatest theorists, scholars, and philosophers ever to have taken pen to paper with thought, and yet here they found themselves having to rehearse the very teachings they claimed to pride themselves on.

It crossed my mind that with pride comes the choice of entitlement. Do we rest on the achievements of yesterday or create today like yesterday never happened? Entitlement fuels both choices. The difference is a matter of perspective.

So what then of the Greek ego? What of an ego that is being squeezed of its money, its pride, and its identity? Which to some extent is mimicked by the experience of every entrepreneur on Earth. My intention was to understand.

It's funny how people attribute the type of hostility associated with the ego to any one body of people or race, playing it aloof to the struggles of a foreign collective. There is no such thing as the Greek ego. The ego is the ego, no matter what nation on earth it resides.

What is funny is that certain groups of humans see themselves different or detached from their human counterparts when the reality is that the ego knows no race, gender, or title. The ego is our in-built robot. In reality, the more egotistical we become, the more we evolve into robots, the easier we are to predict, and the easier we are to play. This notion gave birth to *The Game Entrepreneur*.

Before arriving at the point where I intentionally deployed myself into the twisted egocentricity of Greece, a year of living off my girlfriend's pay cheque in my parents' house, promising them all that I was on to something. I made sure that my ideas were valuable in the real world, if only just to confirm that I was not completely delusional. The way I see it, I sold two and bit years of my life to the second-largest media corporation in the world at a measly $32,000 a year of a company with a yearly earning close to $1.2 billion.

I sold these years because I knew that, when I got to this point, writing my own book and building my own brand, sceptics would say, "Shut up, boy. You don't know anything about anything." And I'd be in a position to politely respond, "What about me, sir or madam, puts you in a derivative of fear?" (chapter 13). The question alone would silence the critics, and I would carry on with the knowledge that my ideas contributed to $200 million worth of insights and strategy for some of the largest brands in the world. Confidence comes from knowing what you're capable of delivering.

Needless to say, I traded two years of my life for knowledge and the confirmation that my ideas could and would sell in the world of business. Furthermore, it is with great pleasure that I embark on my entrepreneurial journey, even trekking through the initial years of poverty, because it seems more of a risk for me to stay in a day job at $32,000 a year than to apply my mind in creating something brand new.

This book is not religiously sanctioned or law abidingly polite and seeks only to endorse current intellectual and spiritual zeitgeist, a very cool word I learnt in my reading journey while prepping for this book. Zeitgeist comes from the German philosopher Georg Wilhelm Friedrich Hegel, in what he referred to as *der Geist sienna Zeit* or *The Spirit of His Day*. The spirit of today embodies change, a new world order: 'for the people by the people'. The masses are realizing their power, and it seems the glue uniting people is neither religious nor political, as much as it is a universal connection to nature and emotion. We are becoming aware of ourselves in time and space, so the future holds the potential for us to refabricate the human condition. The future requires us all to be entrepreneurs, humans who have reinvented their perspective on fear.

I stopped listening for the truth and started listening for the underlying need or want that set out to make something true. I stopped listening to boring interviews with billionaires, probably about the same time I stopped believing in

Christianity as anything more than a remarkably well-told story. I never set out to destroy the line that my parents worked so hard to enforce. I just made it my business to see it differently. Institutions are simply man-made brands.

I am of the opinion that, if the billionaires, politicians, or religious papal, were of any greater good, other than to cater to their own bottom lines, then the world would not be in the dire straits it is today. It is logical that institutions built on fear will set out to create fear. We are individually responsible for the questioning of their motives. The world will not change unless the people in it change first.

Entrepreneurs are the future. Our actions and our thoughts today shape everything coming tomorrow because we are tomorrow's 1 per cent, and I use this example loosely in the hope that a greater consciousness will alleviate the structure of this current hierarchy. Let's face it. Whoever the 1 per cent is today, whether they be the Illuminati, the Simpsons, or an *Eyes Wide Shut* kink group of cray, one thing's for sure. They are probably getting really old, and they have so much money that their kids are more concerned with getting #instafamous.

I have a vision for a better future led by better leaders. I am not in the business of hearing truth or defending it for that matter. I am of the position that truth blatantly does not exist. I'm in the business of creating opportunity. Simple!

*The Game Entrepreneur* is a "get off the grass, wash your face, and listen up" kind of book that requires you to switch on your brain. It's a small book, but it packs a punch. And trust me. It's not for everyone, but for those willing to open their mind, question some stuff, and like really genuinely question stuff, it will be like the future music festival of your life. Welcome to *The Game Entrepreneur*!

Kind Regards,
George Konstand

## Chapter One

# THE GAME

The game is neither for nor against us. We are the players. In the game, we either play or are played. The choice is fundamentally ours. The game is an imagined reality built around an appraisal system that we have come to call business.

This system does not belong to any one of us. It is the medium through which value travels, converting one source of currency into another. The data we feed into the system is evaluated, appraised, and then returned to us as profit or loss, an outcome that we then choose to make our business.

We, the players, infuse outcomes with emotion. We become emotional about processes, falling in love with the system. We are in lust with its money. We seek excitement from the deals it proposes. It becomes the focus of our wildest dreams and worst fears, the allure of wealth and the hate for losing.

It seems absurd how far invested we've become in systems of logic. It's as though we invite the abandonment. From the onset, it is clear that the system is unable to reason with human emotionality, delivering success and failure unrelentingly to players who reason with numbers to derive the meaning of their existence. Yet still we play, caring more about the condition of the game than the way in which we are played by it.

The system was not built to empathise. It was built simply to rationalise the value of human creativity against profit and loss with no love lost. Success and failure are emotional attributes that we, the players, assign to large or small amounts of income because the business of *income* reflects our ego. So, the winning and losing characteristics that we attribute to these numbers reflect how we imagine the world.

The system merely offers an appraisal for whatever data it is fed objectively as profit or loss.

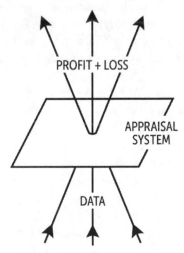

Diagram 1.1. Appraisal system.

The reality of business is that numerical outcomes are dealt back to emotional players, waiting on the other end of the business door, hoping that they will receive an outcome they can declare successful, a rightful reward, or alas a terrible failure. Human subjectivity almost always mars business outcomes.

If the players in the game were robots, they would mechanically declare business outcomes as profit or loss and work tirelessly with an unrelenting appetite for profit. But then the world of business would lose its lustre. How would we feel success if nobody failed?

A critical fact often overlooked by the majority of players, winners and losers combined, is that, without winners and losers, there would be no game. No party. No Gatsby. No *Wolf of Wall Street*. No rush. No race. No hustle. No deal!

Chapter Two

# WINNING AND LOSING, IT'S OUR CHOICE!

We, the players, forget how much control we have over the game. The distinction between what is real and what is imagined has blurred. We have come to perceive the game as reality, needing it more than it needs us. We have come to think of the game as normal and natural. Granted, we were born into it, we know no other way, and at some point, we became preoccupied with living up to the rules of the game rather than actually trying to create them. We've gotten caught up in the binaries: wealth and poverty, success and failure, and winning and losing, the ultimate binary. We forget that we are playing a game.

A game insinuates that we report to either a winning or losing side. We own how well we play. How easily we are played, well, that's just the nature of the game, right? While it seems absurd to think that the rules of a game pre-empt our every natural move, one question remains: Is the allure of winning, however big or small, more important to us than the actual win? How many players are actually winning? 1 per cent? And how many players are measuring their small wins in an overall losing hand?

We gamble with our lives. We are addicted to the bright lights of success, which makes us relentless, chasing big dreams and crushing anything and everything in our path. The feeling is natural and wild. But are we ever actually winning?

The problem is this: To not question the things we perceive to be natural or normal is like trying to build a house on sand and hoping it won't sink. If there is no question of where ideas or rules originate from, then we abide by all of them, naturally and somewhat robotically, which has become normal.

This is where the game gets interesting. Our ability to question and critically analyse the origins of truth that we so blindly abide by awards certain players the right to win over a losing majority. It seems that the only variable between winning and losing players is their mentality, their perspective, that is, a player who is conscious of the nature of the game as opposed to playing the game naturally. Perspective is the difference between playing the game and being played. How's that for a binary?

The game doesn't play anyone. It simply prescribes the rules for play and creates a platform for players to play. We are either reacting or responding to the cards being dealt. So we blame the house that always wins but never accept responsibility for the hand that always loses. At this point, we have to make the conscious decision, to play or be played.

No matter the outcome, the winner chose to win, and the loser subconsciously chose to lose. Whether decisions are made consciously or subconsciously, they belong to their governing bodies. We are responsible for everything good and bad that happens to us. We are accountable for winning or losing.

Appraisal systems grant no trophies to winners and losers. That's something players do to assert their ego. Appraisal systems exist only to evaluate the opportunities that we create. Profit and loss is the endpoint of a purely functional business equation. Understanding this business logic requires an objective perspective. Winning and losing is measured relative to our experience of profit, a completely subjective perspective. Perspective is power in the game. It defines our position.

Choosing to win requires that we reserve emotionality for human engagement, which offers the opportunity to create influence. Influence is currency, as business is the art of selling to humans. There can be no profit without the human decision to invest. Influence and emotionality are only relevant at the pre-appraisal stage of business, where they can affect the profit or loss evaluation.

Objective perspective requires we regulate emotionality. Winning simply requires exercising the ratio of emotion and logic in accordance with the function of an appraisal system in an "Emotion In: Logic Out" ratio.

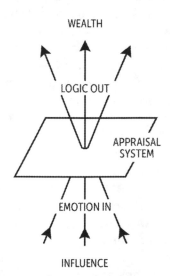

Diagram 2.1. Emotion In: Logic Out ratio.

## Nature of the Game

Aristotle Onassis, a serial Entrepreneur and shipping Tycoon, once said, "The rules are ... there are no rules." And essentially, there really are no rules. A game is imagined to exist with rules, so if we find ourselves playing by rules, then we should question whose game we are playing in.

To play and win is to see beyond the rules we are prescribed to follow. For as long as we abide by rules, we are accepting them as truth. Truth is considered natural and God-given. The only thing natural and God-given inside and outside of the game is nature and all things natural: the universe, animals, living organisms, and the human being who has found itself roaming the planet aimlessly looking for a game to play. Could reality be so basic? Imagine such a basic reality mocking our human complexity. And yet, this is the only thing we know.

The game is a natural fight for survival. After all, that is the nature of our basic seeking habits. Players must understand their innate need to survive. This is the game that nature intends. The question is: How natural is our behaviour after we have satisfied our need to survive?

In the game, a player imagines their success as the measure of value accrued in his or her possessions, but this idea is followed by the most dramatic of all ironies, that is, material possessions have no value. They are only ever depreciating. They exist outside of the fundamental nature of survival; therefore, they are subject to the trending wants and needs of their human owners.

Wealth is the business of subjectivity that we find ourselves playing in after we have established a means to survive. Wealth is the currency of our ego and expressed through the ownership and endorsement of brands in an attempt to define our human form.

Understanding what players want is a matter of understanding how they see themselves. This is also how we come to realise what is relevant to them. Relevance is how we engage humans, influence emotionality and generate value in an "Emotion In : Logic Out" ratio.

Chapter Three

# ENTREPRENEUR, THE PLAYER AMONGST PLAYERS

Entrepreneur, we are in the business of simplicity. If things are not simple, black and white, they are simply obstacles. This notion insinuates that we have a lot of simplifying to do. We have to make the conscious decision to reject how we were taught to think, simplify, and personify a player who possesses a winning entrepreneurial perspective.

In the game, an entrepreneur is the player amongst players. An entrepreneur is defined as someone with a problem-solving perspective, thinking strategically from a natural origin to determine the core of a problem and then providing a relevant solution in the form of a product or service. Entrepreneurialism is the understanding that we can sell solutions. Let us solve problems!

## The Formula: Obstacle - Catalyst = Solution

1. Identify the obstacle.
2. Determine the catalyst or cause(s) of that obstacle.
3. Develop a strategy that rids us of the catalyst and, in turn, the obstacle.

Problem solving, like business, is functional. They are both built on appraisal systems. Why then is problem solving and business often met with so much dysfunction? This is due to the disproportionate areas of knowledge about the business function in relation to the human function, resulting in a lack of clarity when developing an approach to both.

When developing a solution to a problem, we must have a clear understanding of the obstacles standing in our way. Similarly, when developing a solution to a human problem, we cannot possibly visualise the obstacles, if we lack human insight. There are no grounds for developing a winning strategy. As a result, we dilute our approach to business strategy and our intended market and, in turn, dilute our profit outcome. Our lack of insight is often subjectively experienced as failure. If we simply approached the business model with stronger insights, then we'd get better outcomes.

For example, when going to the supermarket, if we know what we're after, we can ask the shop assistant to guide us to a specific aisle and shelf. We can clearly navigate ourselves to a specific location and find the product we're after. The experience is short, sweet and has satisfied our needs. The process is performed with clarity and confidence.

On the other hand, if we do not know what we're looking for, we roam every aisle, look at every product, and convince ourselves that we need things other than the one thing we actually want. The lack of clarity and intention is unproductive. It wastes time and money and leaves us feeling unsatisfied.

Business is the imagined reality in which players exist in the pursuit of creating wealth. But when wealth is the focus of business strategy, then we are only ever taking to outcomes with further outcomes and never actually influencing wealth. (Refer to diagram 2.1.) Creating wealth is never about numbers. It's about influence. Logically, profit and loss can only ever be affected through the "Emotion In" side of the ratio.

Entrepreneurial perspective is a matter of creating influence with an "Emotion In: Logic Out" ratio in mind.

## Chapter Four

# DYSFUNCTIONAL PLAYERS

There is no such thing as dysfunctional business. There are only dysfunctional players in business. Dysfunctional players will seek complexity. Winning players understand that they are in the business of simplicity. Simplicity is the knowledge that we are conditioned to seek complexity. Complexity is: fear of the unknown.

We embrace distractions, overcomplicate situations, and dwell on problems, but not because there is no solution. It's because we have the instinctive foresight to predict that the solution will send us into uncharted territories of the scary unknown. Our fear of the unknown is terrifying. This fear is justified biologically as we are constructed to either fight or take flight from the unknown.

Overcoming our fear of the unknown dissolves the complexity that we surround ourselves with. We must reprogram our minds to understand the unknown as a playing field of opportunity. Here's how: Consider all the things we know and have experienced thus far. Has the known provided us with the opportunity to become the type of people we want to be? Has the known way of life been interesting, freeing, or financially comforting?

Anybody who aspires to achieve something greater than what he or she already has realises that the known is not enough. We must consider the binary that is the known and unknown and question if the known can possibly sustain our intellectual, mental, and emotional state of mind. Can the world as we have known it to be possibly cater to our appetite for creating new and interesting opportunities? For the majority of us entrepreneurs, I think not.

This concludes, in the mentality of problem solving, that the unknown holds every possibility to create our dreams and ideas and is the key to everything that is new and amazing in this world. Fear, or that gut-wrenching feeling of being scared, functions with dual purpose, either to keep us in our known comfort zones or fuel an aspirational vigour that seeks out opportunities in the unknown. All of a sudden, the unknown is a positive realm of opportunity and adventure, and fear is an indicator for opportunity.

In saying that, fearlessness does not exist. It is a virtue held by the demigods we read about in mythology. Reprogramming our minds to see fear as an indicator of opportunity is a virtue, understood by a very real and successful entrepreneur.

First, we must accept the fundamental nature of fear. Fear is a gift. Like all systems within the human body, fear has its place. It functions as a detector of the unknown. We must consider how we have been taught to react to the presence of fear. When we live idle within fear, its mechanic controls us. It detects the unknown and alerts us to retreat. Like an animal in an electric cage, every time we touch the cage, we receive a shock and dramatically pull back into the safety of our nook.

Reacting to fear (detector of the unknown) keeps us in the known. Living in the known by default of fear results from a lack of insight into our own humanity and the nature of our emotionality, we choose to stay within the comforts of the known because it is safe. We sacrifice opportunity for safety. Living in the known requires the condition of tolerance that restricts our freedom, like in the example of the animal in the cage. We should question: Are we ever really safe living in that electric cage, or are we conditioned to tolerate it in the name of comfort at the expense of our freedom?

Tolerance is why we adhere to rules. And not surprisingly, every institution that profits from our obedience teaches it. In rejection of the unknown, we make the decision to dwell in a problem without the initiative to identify it or provide a relevant solution. Tolerance is the deflection of responsibility and accountability in the name of safety.

As much as fear can cage us in, it can work equally to free us. Fear is neither good nor bad. It is a natural gift, a tool given to us to survive. Perspective is everything. Fear is functional. It alerts us to new and unknown data from the outside world. How we identify this data is a matter of perspective.

If we refuse to assess new data objectively, then we cannot accurately assess if it is truly a threat or an opportunity because we only ever read new data as different from us and attach it with all the misconceptions of difference: bad, abnormal, evil, and the other. How can we possibly trust our gut instinct in business if it is always telling us to deflect the unknown and seek out the known? Are we throwing opportunities out the window because we have been taught to mimic the saying "Trust your gut instinct"?

Entrepreneurs recognise fear as the discomfort we feel when we are comfortable. Fear is the anxiety and unease within us that tells us we can be doing more. Fear makes us feel like we're wasting away. It's the want to be ambitious. It's the pursuit of something bigger that will not allow us to simply be. Our fear receptors detect opportunity, and we are alerted to the danger of staying in the known at risk of missing this opportunity.

Innovation starts where complexity ends. We must disarm ourselves of dysfunction: bad relationships, unloving people, and situations that we keep in place because they reflect our insecurities. For as long as we tolerate problematic people and circumstances, we invite dysfunction. Dysfunction is the opposite of clarity. It kills entrepreneurial perspective.

Invite clarity. Clarity incites a shift in perspective. We must make a conscious decision to live the life we have imagined, actively choosing to be the beginning and the end of our own story. The player who wins is open to ideas and opportunities. Fear does not cage us in.

## Chapter Five

# THE BIOLOGY OF ENTREPRENEURIALISM

Understanding our biological responses to fear is the secret to reprogramming our minds. This involves developing a sense of objective clarity that allows us to pull back from a situation and look at it from a clear and functional perspective. Perspective is the difference between responding and reacting.

We are led to believe that we have progressed far beyond our primate ancestors. After all, we are abundantly equipped with superior technology, culture, and literature: iPhones, tablets, planes, skyscrapers, Shakespeare, and all the rest. And yet, when the unknown or the other confronts us, we instantly regress, reacting with the same primitive receptors that we had imagined our modern selves to be so far removed from.

We are biologically programmed to reinvent our future from our past. We are programmed to mimic experiences that conform to old ways of being because the old is comfortable. They are known ways of receiving the world. Fear has the capability of manipulating our future experiences to mimic experiences from our past, allowing us to exist a lifetime, comfortably in a reality that we know.

While it is true that we are the creators of our own reality, it is an undeniable fact that the reality we seek to create is subject to the clarity of our mind from which we project our wants and needs.

As human beings, everything we experience is emotional. We are programmed to understand the world emotionally before we understand it logically. But at some point, we must accept responsibility for the logical assessment—or lack thereof—of our emotional experiences.

## The Known and Unknown

Humans respond to the unknown with the perception of an imminent threat. The secretion of adrenalin in fight-or-flight response tells us to run, run hard, and run fast, seeking shelter and protection. We experience the unknown with feelings of being threatened and having pain, sorrow, and abuse before we can logically analyse what it actually is, something new. A majority of players will react to their emotional interpretation of the unknown by taking flight. Very few players will endure the temporarily heightened state of stress and adapt to new environments.

In a 2013 TEDx Youth presentation Dr. Jill Bolte Taylor[2], an American Neuroanatomist, gave a powerful talk about mindfulness "as the process of observing our bodies neurocircuitry to understand experiences from within and outside of the body (1:31)." Dr. Taylor states, "We have the ability to change the thoughts in our brains, to pick and choose what's going on inside our heads, and ultimately control what we are projecting into the perceptive world (1:42)." Overcoming fear is a process of mindfulness that takes ninety seconds of consciousness. "Ninety seconds is all the time needed to flush out the adrenalin, shot into our bodies during the initiation of fight-or-flight response (2:42)." Though we are momentarily left in a panic "or a declared state of self-preservation (5:38)," we still have access to "higher cortical thinking and an ability to consciously reassess situations (6:05)" in a process of learning.

The player who maintains his or her poker face is always able to develop a logical understanding of an unknown situation. An awareness of our internal human function gives us greater insight into why we project certain subjectivities and similarly the thought process behind why others react and respond. These rare players possess an objective clarity that is the key to entrepreneurial perspective.

A want to learn new things and seek out opportunities that are completely contrary to one's known experience mark entrepreneurial perspective. This generally explains why a good lot of us insist on jumping out of planes and/ or spaceships in some cases. We are of the few who have learnt to befriend the butterflies.

Mindfulness is relevant to how we conduct ourselves in business. The mentality driving us into business is also the same mentality destroying our dreams. Here's why: Our ego manifests itself in the form of an emotional territory that lives in our brain, our comfort zone. Fear protects this territory. The brain activates fight-or-flight responses in an attempt to preserve its known territory.

For as long as we allow it, our brain will perceive everything from within our comfort zone as prior life experiences have mapped out. This is why we judge people, experiences, and events in relation to known and unknown formats of normality that we have nurtured over time. How do you feel when you meet somebody who has the same name as your ex-partner?

We are conditioned to dwell in our ego and project our wants and needs from it. We imagine our reality from within it and build our identity based on it. From the comforts of our known territory, our ego seeks out everything we want in the material world.

Through the ego, we identify our self-worth, entitlement, or failure and seek to create a sense of identity. We project this identity into the world through our association with brands and like-minded people, who similarly reflect our emotional predisposition, asserting an imagined sense of self.

Our ego perceives everything it encounters from a series of learnt truths, a set of cultural, traditional, religious, and political values that it has come to resonate with throughout life experience. The ego is set to judge all incoming data against these prescribed truths and values.

The ego tells us to align ourselves with the products that best represent how we feel about ourselves. This is the driving force behind 'why'. For example, a young male entrepreneur may seek out a brand like Tom Ford because he identifies with that "Jay-Z/Justin T" kind of swagger that says "I'm all party on the outside and business in the brain!" Or it's similarly how a child will demand a McDonald's Happy Meal at the first sight of those golden arches because there is something about the colours, toys, and a friendly clown that a young ego seeks out, to identify, the nature of their playfulness.

Entrepreneurial perspective is recognizing why we seek out the people, situations, and brands that we do. We are either driving decisions consciously or being driven by them subconsciously.

## Chapter Six

# THE EGO AT PLAY

Understanding the ego at play is the key to winning the game. In more of a play strategy, the ego can be used as a tool for mindful play within the game. Objectifying our ego is a matter of understanding reason. We defend and project our wants and opinions from territories we *know* the same way others do. Therefore, if we seek to understand what others *know*, we can begin to understand what they want and how they perceive. This is what it means to "know thyself."

Emotional objectivity sheds light on player subjectivity, which otherwise distorts a player's reality. A subjective player perceives the world completely relative to his or her emotional territory, his or her ego. A subjective player is delusional, constantly mimicking the values that they have come to know as truth.

For example, if a player grows up in an environment where he or she was abused and has experienced abandonment by their parent or protector, then they are emotionally destined to seek out and create abuse and abandonment in their future relationships. The only way a player can steer themselves away from the known comfort of such abuse is to understand that they seek it out.

Reasoning with what we know gives us diplomacy. In that, we are not always right, and our beliefs are not truth. Our wants, needs, and motivations can at times be more destructive than they are productive.

The game must be approached with a strong game face, an objective understanding of the experiences and relationships that in the past and at present conspire to create our ideas of self. Objectivity creates a platform for forgiveness. It is the realization that there is no such thing as truth. There is only the measure of experience against prescribed lessons of wrong and right, that we perceive to be true.

Chapter Seven

# FINDING FREEDOM IN A BRAND

Player ego essentially drives the game. The ego seeks out brands and players who mimic its imagined self. This is how niche markets come into formation. Common values unite groups of players, and they see themselves as equal to or defined by the players and brands they surround themselves with. Common values stem from common emotional territories. Hence, it's why niche markets often form around similar socioeconomic and ethnic backgrounds, age, and contextual similarities.

In the game, the only way to communicate with these groups of like-minded (niche) players is to inspire them with an idea that speaks to the comforts of their emotional territory, inspiring the way they imagine themselves to exist. We do this through a platform called a Brand.

A brand is an idea. We have an opportunity to create a world around an idea as we choose to imagine it, define it, package it, and sell it. A brand can bridge the gap between product and consumer by establishing common values. A brand shapes the way a player receives the world because he or she now perceives the world through the brands vision. They judge the world from the brand's truths and values. Players will perceive the world differently because of the way a brand inspires their imagination. Branding is where a brand and its intended market come together in a way that creates meaning. A player now takes to the world with newfound ideologies inspired by the brand.

For example, take the Kardashian brand. The Kardashians are famous for being pretty. There is no denying how they use their pretty brand to create products to materialise an imagined Kardashian reality. Believe it or not, the Kardashian brand helped shape meaning in the world. They marked the explosion of the booty phenomenon. Their brand stood for an anti-Barbie ideology, in a post-Paris Hilton era. The revival of brunette beauty and all the terminology that created an army of dolls! #Bible Keeks and her krew really kreated a whole new diskourse (of bad spelling)!

If we begin to consider the world from the perspective of branding, we can isolate every single piece of knowledge and experience as an article of branded content. Everything understood to be truth by a player stems from branded ideology. We live in a society constructed on truth, which means we live in a society built on brands who set out to make their ideas come true. Culture celebrates the teaching of truth through judgement of right and wrong, helping to shape cultural expectations that build norms into a society. Judgement of right from wrong is the fabric from which laws are cut out, affecting our overarching worldviews. Law is commonly based on the moral and ethical teachings of religious doctrine and celebrated traditionally through a decree of righteousness over a statement of anti-right and anti-social wrongness. Political and religious brands often share common values and seek to strengthen their influence by endorsing one another through partnership.

We subconsciously enclose ourselves into categories that define who we are, what we deem to be socially acceptable, and what is taboo. In essence, we restrict our ability to imagine because we choose to believe in brands as being real and true as opposed to seeing them as constructs of truth. Constructs are not God-given, and they certainly are not natural the way we choose to imagine them to be.

Every single one of us dwells within an imagined reality.

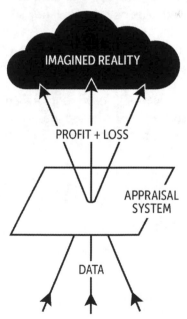

Diagram 7.1. Imagined reality.

Ideas create meaning. They also create truth (for those who believe enough in them). In fact, everything we know is simply an idea. Think about the ideas that shape our reality: our name, age, gender, nationality, religion, favourite sporting team, and so forth. Ideas are created like clouds in the sky. They exist, and we experience them, but they are not a true reflection of reality.

For example, dark clouds create meaning. We presume that it will rain at some point. They shape the way we behave. We may dress differently or choose to carry an umbrella. They can even affect our emotions. We become grumpy and uncomfortable. Some may feel depressed. Dark clouds shape how we perceive experience and are often reflected in our moods with feelings of melancholy or nostalgia.

Dark clouds are an illusion. They are droplets of water clustered together in the sky that float between us and a perfectly sun-filled, blue sky. And yet they shape how we feel and experience the day. Like clouds, ideas affect our lives. Only they are not natural. They are man-made. How well we can identify ideas or brands that shape our experiences determine how well we play the game.

Entrepreneurial perspective requires we are conscious of our relationship with man-made ideas.

Entrepreneurial perspective is about how objective we can be about objects.

## Chapter Eight

# GAME ON!

Entrepreneur, let's do what we do best. Strategise! Strategic thinking in business goes hand in hand with problem solving. Both require us to be adaptable to new information and be receptive to change. Innovation and creation is only really innovative and creative when it is relevant and applicable.

We can only afford the opportunity to create in business if we are creating to satisfy a want or need for a particular group of niche players. Speaking to niche players requires us to understand how they perceive themselves and, in turn, the world, responding to these views with solutions.

In order to engage a niche group of players, we must have solid insights into the influences and institutional brands that already shape the way they perceive. We must understand their way of thinking, their reason, in order to engage with them in a relevant way. Insights should feed into the core of every brand as a way of inviting relevant conversations. It's like going to a black tie event. You cannot expect to get let in with shorts and a T-shirt. You will be outcast and rejected. Think relevance!

## The Game Strategy

Strategic thinking can be broken down to a simple formula:
Vision - Obstacle = Challenge

- **Vision:** Create a valuable brand.
- **Obstacle:** "I'm not sure if my brand is relevant?"
- **Challenge:** Immerse yourself in your niche market. How do they think? How do they feel about the world? Seek to align your brand vision with their aspirations.

## Case Study: The Rubik's Cube (Imagined Reality vs. Reality)

The Rubik's Cube case study is an analogy that best describes how players are produced by brands and, in turn, are shaped to receive the world in a particular way. The Rubik's Cube is an example of how one idea with multiple truths built into it can shape human meaning through experience.

When manufacturing the Rubik's Cube, it exists as an object, a black, rotatable box with six blank sides, equal in meaning.

Diagram 8.1. Black Rubik's Cube.

The simple black box transitions to its next phase, where each side is given a colour. These colours are now infused with meaning and contain truth, albeit assumed truth, where we, the players, know that the objective of the game is to re-coordinate the blue with the blue, red with the red, and so forth because that's the aim of the game, right! Each colour holds a different feeling of belonging. As a collective, they represent an idea, the Rubik's Cube. The colours outline the emotional parameters of the game.

We begin the game with strong determination. We are optimistic that we'll be able to conquer the task. Three minutes pass. We're challenged. The rush of optimism has not yet worn off. Success is still seemingly possible. Six minutes pass. We're getting impatient. The determination is turning into frustration. We start doubting our own capabilities. We are having feelings of failure and becoming conscious of the time we're wasting. Eight minutes pass. The cube goes flying across the room. We're pissed off and hurl abuse at the damn thing. "What a stupid game. What a waste of time. I hate this damn thing. Never again!"

In eight minutes, we go from determined to frustrated and annoyed, having feelings of failure because of a game that we now belittle and call stupid and silly (which, in fact, is a projection of how we have been made to feel). The game has affected us in such a way that we now have resentment against the brand of the Rubik's Cube. "Never again!"

The Rubik's Cube is a metaphor for a brand and the many ideologies collectively built into it to create meaning. Like the game of business, we create meaning about ourselves and the world around us as a result of being produced by a collective of brands.

The game has the ability to emotionally affect its players because the players accepted that the rules are truth. (In the case of the Rubik's Cube, blue must match with blue, red with red, and so forth.)

Truth exists with the understanding that certain values are natural and unquestionable, as opposed to preconceived ideologies that we have been subjected to and in turn come to believe. We must realise that, if we commence with a set of unquestionable truths, the mission to win the game is impossible because we allow ourselves to be marginalised by these truths, those that are imagined into existence by other players who set out to make their ideas come true. So we are being played.

If we take a step back and look beyond the colours (or prescribed truths), we then become inventors or re-inventors of truth. It is all about perspective. Why do we force ourselves to play by the rules when the rules don't actually exist? We imagine that with play there exists prescribed rules. We have been conditioned to expect one from the other, and as a result, we invite the rules because it is easier to colour within the lines on a page than it is to create on a blank canvas with no direction. We abide by laws and religious commandments taught to us from childhood. We believe in their ideologies as unquestionable truths. These truths make up the vast network of institutional brands that create meaning in our lives: wrong and right, desirable and undesirable, and normal and abnormal.

French theorist Michel Foucault (1926–1984) referred to institutions as discourses (brands) that work to produce discursive truth (reason). Foucault proposed the notion that humans are produced and therefore exist within political, religious, and cultural discourses. Humans learn truth as nature, as opposed to nurture, and therefore set out to defend what they know over questioning what is taught as knowledge, resulting in a self-regulating human being. This creates a human condition that confines knowledge to constructs of truth, serving only to benefit the freedom of the institution that created that truth. Ultimately, humans serve as able bodies that police themselves, and others, to sustain social order, implement hierarchy, and maintain a productive working class, what Michel Foucault refers to as biopower.[3]

Capitalism is a brand, an economic discourse that embodies the idea of endless opportunity, wealth, and happiness. As an idea, capitalism awards self-regulating human beings the power to exist unregulated and, in doing so, creates the ultimate playground for humans, playing to outdo one another, captured so satirically in the 1983 film *Scarface*. "The world is yours." Capitalism alludes to notions of freedom and happiness through wealth, attainable by all players. Sure, it affords us the opportunity to do so, if and only when we can overcome the rules that serve to create a self-regulating product of capitalism. Essentially, freedom is a choice, awarded to those who consciously choose it. The thing about consciousness is that it is only attainable outside of judgement.

So what then of a capitalist idea that promotes judgement? I wonder if that's why it fits so well with political and religious discourses, which also set out to create judgement via binaries of wrong and right, good and evil, and rich or poor.

"So what of judgement?" you might ask.

Judgement is the tool we use to entertain the known and reject the unknown. Let us play with words here. Judgement is the tool we use to entertain the past and reject opportunity. Again, judgement is the tool we use to entertain comfort and reject discomfort. Finally, judgement is what we use to protect the known because we innately fear the unknown. How can a capitalist discourse promote opportunity when it teaches us to fear it at the same time? Is opportunity then only awarded to those who break the rules?

Capitalism is a game. Only those willing to question the rules can play for keeps. It is an idea that promotes judgement and teaches fear to regulate how players play. We can only win if we consciously choose to do so. That's what makes playing fun.

For example, while growing up, I would play Monopoly with my siblings and cousins. I would always insist on playing the banker. Not only did I put up the valid argument that I was the eldest and best mathematician, but I would call "shotgun" on it. Naturally, with all that access to cash, it didn't take much for me to shun the rules, often sneaking a five-hundred-dollar note or two or three into my bundle of cash. I had fast hands, and there was never any accusation as I was always handing out money and preaching about how I was the smartest player in the game. Not only was I the biggest cheat, I was also the biggest enforcer of the rules, the moral high-hatter, so to speak. I would insist on playing fair. The rules kept the players in line, and I was happy to enforce them and break them at the same time, as I was of the mindset that it was just a game. So I never let the rules stand in the way of my play.

This type of game play is not restricted to our childhood memories unfortunately. It is simulated in the adult version of the very same game. It seems that those who enforce the rules clearly don't abide by them. You don't have to look too far to find examples, especially when we have politicians using union credit cards to pay for play, I mean, prostitutes. You and I know exactly what I mean. Then again, politicians and prostitutes seem to be synonymous as they are constantly playing the same game of money, power, greed, and lust. The difference between the two is the integrity of the profession. Integrity only ever derives from honesty, which leaves prostitutes as the inevitable winners. There's never any confusion about what they do. What I have done here, is simply connect common brand values.

Winning players are mindful of their position in the game at all times and are also aware of those seemingly righteous players trying to enforce the rules that they themselves rarely adhere to. A player can never assume the integrity of another player in the game, but we can certainly question the nature of the truthful lies he or she tells.

## Chapter Nine

# JUDGEMENT DAY

Like in the example of the Rubik's Cube, a player measures his or her success and failure based on their experience of the game. It's important to note that a willingness to learn marks success. Losing says more about our willingness to learn than it does about the game.

Imagine somebody in this day and age trying to convince you that the earth is flat. Imagine how hell-bent you'd be in arguing the facts with that person. "It's a proven fact that the earth is round!" You'd think that person was completely stupid and unintelligent, and the sight of them would probably begin to frustrate you. "What a dumb thing to say!" Right?

Now, consider we flipped the table. What if we were back in the centuries before Christ and you and everybody else absolutely believed that the earth was flat? And then some dude called Aristotle, turns to you and says, "Hey! Do you know that the world is a ball?" You'd probably look at him like he was a moron and argue with the same conviction you showed in the first part of this example. Little do you realise he's proposing the paradigm of a spherical earth[4].

The point I am trying to make is that, for as long as we think we know something, we do not question it. We believe in it as God-given truth, and we are more than willing to fight for it. The things we choose to believe and what is actually believable are two different things. Imagine the vast difference in perspective. Losing players look out at a sunset and watch their dreams sink into the horizon with the sun. Winning players know that the horizon is an illusion that doesn't actually exist and the sun carries their goals on and on and into tomorrow. The ego will always look to pass on responsibility and blame fate or luck for its lack of opportunity because it is preoccupied catering to the comforts of our known world, deflecting anything that questions the familiar.

We are only ever as successful as the type of story we attempt to write about ourselves. Question the nature of truth! Always!

As entrepreneurs, we sacrifice forty-hour weeks for eighty-hour weeks because creativity has no concept of time. Why can entrepreneurs engage in ancient ways of doing business, such as barter or the exchange of nonmonetary service for service? Why do entrepreneurs seek each other out and share skill sets across industries, crowdsource, and build communities through collaboration?

I would like for this to be the future of the world, and I ask for it blatantly because not asking for the things we want ensures we'll never get them. The nature of today's landscape means that our success and failure is measured on the strength and integrity of our personal and professional brands. The thing about consciousness, whether it's conscious business or personal enlightenment, is that it is built on the fundamental notion that all living matter is connected metaphysically to one natural and intangible source, the universe. With this simple reality, all tangible things lose their value, and all we have left as humans is the ability to emotionally affect one another with our message. Affect the game with our brand.

For a winning (objective) player, there is only his or her brand(s) and endless opportunity. For a losing (subjective) player, there are the rules and the players who set them. Subjectivity is neither productive nor valuable to an entrepreneur seeking to build a valuable brand.

If we play the game with our ego, whether we win, fail, or quit, the only certainty is that we have wasted a lot of time and money being played by another player. So long as we are not playing by our own rules, we are playing by somebody else's. Winning in the game requires a player's conscious decision to do so.

A conscious decision requires objective clarity and a fundamental natural origin that outweighs all other fabricated truths, that of consciousness. Humans have a common origin of knowledge, that is, nothing actually exists or has a name. Everything is created and/or given a name by somebody who imagined it to exist and was great at selling their idea. This is a winning perspective.

Perspective is the difference between winning and losing. Winning is to create an idea that invents truth because we know nothing to be true. Losing is to play the game with truth because we imagine ideas to be true. We must comprehend that we either consciously or subconsciously choose to win or lose. We choose to either invent ideas or abide by them. Play or get played. This is the game.

The instant we recognise our position in the game— and the network of ideas that have come together to form our modern ways of being—is the moment we choose to become winning players. Our ability to objectify the world around us makes us aware of the game in play and all the other players similarly being produced by it or producing it.

We are responsible for everything good and bad that happens to us in our lives. This is because we either consciously or subconsciously chose it. Winning the game requires the conscious decision to do so.

## Case Study: "Know Thyself"

The game becomes apparent when we consider the writing is in our DNA. Losers make the conscious decision to lose, and for the players who choose to win, they cannot help but see the humour in this very notion, considered how absurdly obvious and readily available the teachings are.

The Ancient Greek (Delphic) maxim, GNŌTHI SAUTON, was inscribed on the forecourt wall of the Temple of Apollo at Delphi. It was a gift for all to see there in broad daylight for the consideration of all who passed it, a teaching that said GNŌTHI SAUTON (Know Thyself). Those who take the time to know themselves will live as kings of their own world. These same kings will enslave those who do not.

# ΓΝΩΘΙ ΣΑΥΤΟΝ

Diagram 9.1. Delphic maxim, "Know Thyself."

Imagine the pleasure of seeing GNŌTHI SAUTON to a winning player who understood its meaning, the irony that the answer to a losing man's woes was there in front of him in the light of day. It is not surprising that such irony gave birth to the binaries of tragedy and comedy. How could one empathise with poverty when the poor man chose to be poor?

This is no different from the modern-day writing on the wall.

Diagram 9.2. All-seeing eye.

This symbol is printed on the face of every dollar bill in the United States of America and is similarly represented, across the globe, through pop culture as a symbol for extreme wealth and power. This symbol says more about the game we play in than it does about any one wealthy alumni group, #Illuminati.

If we deconstruct this symbol, it possesses the exact same teaching of GNŌTHI SAUTON and is as accessible as an inscription on a wall. Not surprisingly, the Founding Fathers of America were more than a little inspired by the Ancient Greeks. Aside from the adoption and their unique rendition of a democratic political system, America depicts aesthetically an overt reference to Ancient Greece with buildings mimicking the Parthenon and cities and whole states named after those in Greece. George Washington is depicted as Zeus. "America! A declaration of the new Atlantis!" It's the American dream. It's a land where men can rise in the likeness of a god in a golden city, a Tinseltown.

It is not surprising that America has come to be one of the strongest nations on Earth. After all, it is built on GNŌTHI SAUTON. The all-seeing eye placed on top of a pyramid is a very real depiction of power and hierarchy, levels of consciousness. The all-seeing eye at the top of the pyramid stands for insight. The few players who possess the greatest insight into themselves and ultimately all of humanity possess the power to manipulate, enslave, and play all those that lack it. Knowledge is power!

Chapter Ten

# WHAT DO WE KNOW?

If business is the art of applying simplicity and simplicity is the knowledge that we are taught to seek complexity, then successful business is simply a matter of what we know. What do we know?

A quote from Plato: The Apology of Socrates[5]

> I thought to myself: I am wiser than this man; neither of us probably knows anything that is really good, but he thinks he has knowledge, when he has not, while I, having no knowledge, think I have not.

Socrates was right on point. In conceding to the fact that he knew nothing, he actually knew more. There is the ultimate underlying truth that everything we know—the names, dates, places, and the truth—is made up. Our claim to truth exists outside of a conscious body of knowledge.

We are grossly misled to believe that we, human beings, are vastly complicated and unique to everything and everyone in the world. This is a completely delusional way of thinking. In fact, it is such a wildly delusional notion that it actually supports the conditioning methods of institutional fear. We are led to believe that we are individual and unique while simultaneously being taught that we are one thing and everybody else is the other. Innately, we are being taught to fear what we do not know. We are being taught to fear the unknown, that is, to fear opportunity.

The implicit disconnect that we are led to believe, namely that we are unique individuals, drives us into the comfort of organizational sameness and actively unifies groups and communities in the form of niche markets. If everybody thinks they are different, then they are actually thinking the same. Our inherit uniqueness is a capitalist ideology that works to create humans that are predictable, regimented, and controllably diverse. I will explain why.

Today's human is so tightly wound around institutional ideologies that we have become defensive and politically correct about ideas that we do not even dare question them out of fear of sparking a debate. Have you ever heard, "There are two things you do not talk about, politics and religion"? Well, why the hell not? For as long as we do not question things, we will believe in them blindly. Capitalism has provided us with a product and a brand for every want and every need, so our ego thrives in a relentless pursuit of identity and uniqueness defined by products.

It's ironic that this action is not at all unique to any human. Actually, it makes humans relatively easy to predict. The pursuit of uniqueness is not unique, so to any one person willing to observe, we can see patterns of behaviour, reaction, response, perception, and even choice. In marketing, we refer to humans in categories, kind of like caged chickens:

socially aware, visible achievement, young optimism, real conservatism, look at me, conventional family life, traditional family life, a fairer deal, something better, and basic needs.[6] For the record, "young optimism" refers to the free-range entrepreneurial types. These groups are defined as niche markets or a group of people unified by similar experiences driven by equally similar material wants and needs.

Ideas of nationalism and cultural sameness, shaping self-identity, further categorise and unify humans. Nationalism is a brand story of how we came to be Australian, American, English, and so forth. Identifying ourselves with a nation allows us to adopt an identity that is fabricated and instructs how we should behave according to what is and isn't acceptable.

For example, I was born and raised in Australia; therefore, Australian ideologies, the Australian dream, multiculturalism, and values such as mateship influence my identity. Similarly, I identify with the Australian brand: the flag, the national anthem, the kangaroo, the history of the native Aboriginal people, Captain Cook, Ned Kelly, Vegemite, and so forth. Political and educational institutions teach these ideologies, and the media dispenses them.

Like Australia, every nation of the world uses the same method of teaching ideologies to define its country and people, drawing a line in the sand that says, "This is one nation, and all that is foreign is the other. This is ours, and that is theirs!"

If politics had it that we went to war tomorrow, we could justify the murder of human beings, in the name of nationalism and patriotism, ideologies that define and distinguish between you and I, respectively. Ironically, this binary is constructed by a man or woman, no more or less capable to do so than you or I, with one distinct difference. They had an idea, and they were great at selling it.

Choice is a virtue only awarded to those who utilise the power of fear as the detection of opportunity instead of being caged in by it. If we are subjective about fear, then fear will become our inability to conform to our natural state of universal sameness. Our ego will not have it. The ego will violently resist its nature. The unknown is hell for our ego. We prefer to accept mediocrity in a material world than to accept a metaphysical reality that gives us the power to create whatever we imagine.

This very notion is so overwhelming and overflowing with possibility, like a blank canvas. No lines on the page. The unknown is terrifying for a player invested in their subjectivities. In their mind, they have everything to lose.

Ego-driven players welcome complexity to fill up all the space: poisonous relationships, short-term satisfaction, phones and tablets, more and more and more information. It's the endless pursuit of perfection. It's complexity.

If a player cannot see their own ego at play, they cannot possibly see through the ego of another player. They have no way of empathizing with that player because they are preoccupied defending what they know.

## Chapter Eleven

# GAME PLAN

Entrepreneur, we are not in the business of complexity. Nor are we in the business of infinite perplexity. I do not suggest a fruitless pursuit of nothingness. We are in business after all. But understanding our universal sameness as the binding matter that connects us with our competitors, consumers, investors, and partners allows us to objectify emotion in a way that we can begin to have more real and relevant conversations. Being aware of our universal sameness relieves us of our subjective self. We realise that there is nothing special or different about our individual emotions, so they do not consume us. This invites a sense of calm, an ability to disarm emotions that cause complexity and dysfunction. This invites clarity.

Ironically, inviting in our universal sameness and rejecting the ego or our ideas of self—uniqueness, difference, and irregularities—asserts a calmness that is in fact unique, different, and irregular in an otherwise subjective world. The act of seeking out our natural origin opens up paths of communication, inspires creativity and innovation, and attracts opportunity.

Prescribed truths or invented rules cannot define or marginalise universal sameness. When we possess the ability to understand humanity from a point of sameness and our metaphysical connection to everything living, we then possess the power of love, forgiveness, and empathy.

Empathy is the key tool for seeking out emotional insights from humans. Insights are the foundation of every moneymaking idea ever sold or created because, when true emotional insights are written into a brand message, they resonate with their particular audience.

Understanding our core audience from within their comfort zone is the key to creating, innovating, and selling with relevant messaging. Relevance is the key to influence. Influence is currency in business. Coming to understand these business functions is the key to winning in the game.

Becoming influential is essentially a case of understanding and creating relevant brands and products, as opposed to flooding the market with complex gadgets and sexy logos that simply do not resonate with any particular market. We have a very real opportunity now to create a valuable brand. As entrepreneurs, it is critical that we start lean. We must use the tools around us to test and trial ideas. We have the tools to propel ideas into the world and test how they are received. Social landscapes invite direct conversations with real people, consumers, investors, and partners. There is nothing standing in the way of us creating something epic, being about something, and inspiring like-minded people now.

So, where do we start?

## Chapter Twelve

# BUILD A BRAND. PLAY IT YOUR WAY!

A brand is a name that represents an idea in its entirety. Branding is the human experience of that idea. Logos, trademarks, symbols, and colours are not branding. They are simply logos, trademarks, symbols, and colours that indicate we are about to engage with a particular idea.

A brand may represent our personal identity, a product, or a service, but the name attributed to its entity does not define it. The emotional sentiment that has come to resonate with its name after humans have experienced it defines a brand.

A brand requires that we be about something, that is, we stand for a particular idea. When asked, "What is it that you do?" the actual question is, "What idea are you selling?" Our response should be clear and concise, short, and to the point. We have to make people fall in love with us quickly.

To do this, we have to get over ourselves (our ego) and be about them. If they have to ask, "What is it that you do," they already anticipate that you're selling something. Do you know how salespeople are perceived? Go out and see. You will have a good laugh!

By all means, know your brand and talk to people about it. But building influence is about having conversations first, intriguing people with your personality, and then telling them about your ideas as they appear in your brand.

Building value in business is about finding the people who our brand would mean the world to and understanding that group of people better than they understand themselves. This is the secret to being relevant. Relevance sells our brand without the sales pitch because it speaks to the wants and needs of a niche market. Achieving relevance requires that we tie insights into our ideas. A brand that speaks to the subjectivities of its niche market is on point with price, product, promotion, and place.

Insights come in the form of statistical (quantitative) and emotional (qualitative) information from the humans dwelling within a target market. Quantitative insights determine where, when, and how to approach a niche market. This is where you will find them, when is the best time to speak to them, and which media channels they are most receptive to.

Qualitative insights refer to the emotional underpinnings of a niche market: what and why. These are the likes, dislikes, wants, needs, values, beliefs, and aspirations of our niche market, subject to their contextual influences: people, places, events, and time.

What is the key to positioning our brand in the right light and to the right people? If we cannot understand the truth behind why a niche market has come to think and feel the way it does, then we cannot speak to its why. Seek to understand your niche from the inside out. This is how your brand becomes relevant.

## A Brand

A brand is an idea that exists as the inventor of truth. A brand represents a vision. It says, "I believe in this. I stand for this, and this is why." Consumers resonate with particular ideas because they share common values. Values can be best described as adjectives or describing words that we use to express feelings of self in an attempt to define and create meaning. The ego will set out to adopt ideas that best reflect how players imagine themselves to exist. Brand endorsement is an extension of player identity and the construct from which we measure and defend truth.

## Brand Experience

Brand experience is the creator of perception. An idea creates a platform for learning. Learning is the process of categorizing and defining experience to arrive at truth. A brand shapes or confirms particular thoughts or beliefs and is projected into the imagination of the consumer, affecting how they perceive the world.

## Identity and Perception

The ego defines itself through association with material things (brands) and projects those brand values in order to materialise innate concepts of self. For example, a woman spends two thousand dollars on a Louis Vuitton bag. The bag is like any other well-crafted leather piece of hand luggage. That woman is not purchasing the bag for its functionality. She is purchasing it because she perceives herself to be aligned with the values of Louis Vuitton: classic elegance, attention to detail, luxury, and wealth. As a winning player, we must analyse how certain product brands contribute to the fabrication of human identity. Consumer trends mimic the human experience of the world.

## Branding

Perception is the creator of an imagined reality or an illusion. Everything we know to be real and true is an illusion. An illusion is a projection of all things learnt through experience. It is the space that we imagine ourselves to exist within, a projection of all our truths, values, and aspirations.

Illusions are built on judgement, the combined perception of self and the world around us, to form an opinion that says, "Yes, this is what I am about" or "No way! That's not me." Everything we claim to know is actually not knowledge. It's an adoption of brand values as truth and I am of the opinion that truth blatantly does not exist.

## The Game Illusion

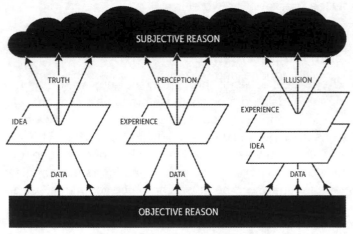

Diagram 12.1. The game illusion.

Our position in the game depends on how we perceive truth. The game illusion is the conversion of objective reason to subjective reason, the mindset that man-made ideas produce truth, shaping the nature of play.

Subjective reason requires players to accept that they are small enough to be defined by the brands they experience, renouncing their connection to universal sameness. Objective reason puts the game into perspective as an illusion. Truth does not restrict players who understand objective reason. They are of the mindset that they can invent brands that create truth. Our position is purely reliant on our relationship with fear.

Entrepreneur, nothing exists. You choose! A brand is an opportunity to influence players within the game illusion. Humans believe in truth because they fall in love with ideas and come to think of these ideas as saying something about their character. Thus, they choose to endorse these ideas, defend them, and uphold their values. Ideas are only relevant to humans when they share common values. If a brand shares the values of its niche market, then emotionally, the humans within that niche, are conditioned to read the brand as known and respond to it with love.

The declaration of known data triggers the release of dopamine within the brain. Dopamine is recognised as a reward hormone and is attributed to feelings of safety. Safety is attributed also to love, an emotion reserved for one's comfort zone.

Let's try to understand a player from within their comfort zone.

## Chapter Thirteen

# THE PLAYER

The game is the art of influencing players. Players are human, and for as long as we are selling to humans, we must recognise that the game is the business of making humans fall in love with ideas. The way we experience brands is tied to our emotionality, and we naturally attribute brands with very human characteristics.

Brands are very much judged in the same way that we judge people. If we like them and they speak our language, we fall in love. Brand experience simulates human engagement: the first impression, affection, trust building, advocacy, and/ or defence. As ideal as it sounds to separate business from pleasure, we are not very good at it. Feelings drive and motivate us, and it's impossible to detach ourselves from the things we feel, especially if we cannot derive reason for why we feel them. "I love it. I don't know why. I just do!" or "I get a bad feeling. It just doesn't feel right!"

Our known and unknown formats of experience guide the gut feelings that render brands as valuable or invaluable. A positive experience is one that we perceive to resonate with our known territory and can result in lifelong advocacy of a brand. An experience that challenges a player's known territory is perceived as negative and can almost entirely destroy the emotional connection forever. Emotional connections and brand engagement are subject to the known and unknown binaries of self. "I love that." "I hate it."

Building connections is about speaking in the language of your intended market. When selling, we must take one key human insight into account. "Human beings only care about what they want!"[7]

The simplicity of this statement is overwhelming. Entrepreneurs must become masters of their own kind. Our capability to be influential and persuasive comes from understanding why humans do, say, and want the things they do and being empathetic to their reasoning. We must question: What is driving action? What drives an individual to seek out certain things? What are the words escaping them saying about their entire entity? We must become master readers of the human before we can speak to it in a way that is relevant.

Selling is never about drilling products into consumers. It is always about creating a positive relationship with a human that indorses a sale, repeats purchase, and provides positive word of mouth. Selling is about creating a platform that engages human interest and incites a "want to buy."

Brand strategy is developed after we have come to identify human emotional and behavioural tendencies as a matter of functionality—neurological, psychological, and emotional—working together to create reason within and outside of the human being.

## Receiving Information:
## How Experience Functions

Experience is subject to perception. Understanding our niche market's consummatory state of mind requires we assess the fundamental nature of human response to incoming data in a functional way and then apply this nature to a particular context. This is the foundation of the nurtured being.

## The Nervous System

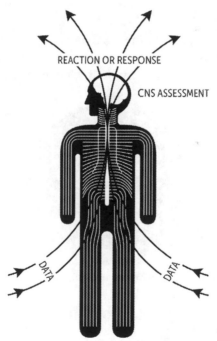

Diagram 13.1. The function of human interpretation and response systems.

The peripheral nervous system (PNS) is the vast network of nerves that connects the body's limbs and organs to the central nervous system (CNS), the spinal cord and the brain. The PNS is made up of the somatic nervous systems (movement and receiving external data) and autonomic nervous systems (fight-or-flight response and rest-and-digest response). These systems carry data to and from the CNS. Once incoming data reaches the CNS, the brain assesses it and rationalises data against known and unknown neurocircuits, activating either a reaction or a response.

## Interpreting Information: How Perception Functions

All data received from the outside world is subject to our learnt truths, prior experiences, and memories, which make up the known and unknown neurocircuits of the brain.

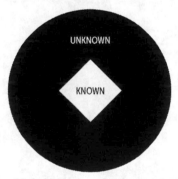

Diagram 13.2. Known and unknown territories.

Known data generates a *response* as it is interpreted as normal. Normality is perceived from within the comfort zone; therefore, the human accepts the data, responding to it with conviction and asserting truth.

Unknown data generates a *reaction*, the brain initiates the primal fight-or-flight response in the PNS, and the human is reactive to the data being presented by the external situation. Unknown data is perceived as a threat to the comfort zone, so the human is prepared to either fight or flee back to their preferred state of comfort. This process allows no further access to higher perceptual parts of the brain as the brain prepares a reaction. This process is completely attributed to fear.

The human body is more robotic than any personality would have us believe. We've established that the player receives a constant flow of data from the world around them. This data is received and interpreted according to our known predisposition, or the territory within our mind that holds our truths and values, shaping how we perceive the world. Known and unknown data in the human brain is similarly declarative of what is perceived to be valuable or invaluable.

The way we position our brand is a matter of seeking out a niche market and understanding what that niche group declares as valuable or invaluable. This is what unites them after all.

## The Psychological Imprint

It is vital that we map out a player's contextual predisposition that currently shapes the way he or she experiences the world. Known data is rationalised against learnt formats of understanding. Childhood and early adult stages of human life determine how we perceive normality. What we constantly experience in early learning stages of life creates patterns of understanding that shape our concept of normal, nurture.

Normal is the imagined territory in which we exist, the illusion that we call reality. Our truths set up the parameters of this territory, marking known and unknown regions. These parameters shape the way we perceive brands, people, the self, and the world around us.

Neurologically, our body is wired to stay within our known comfort zone, so everything we perceive is actually interpreted and projected back into the world as an old response or a mimicked response, like in an infomercial. "Here's a response that we prepared earlier."

Our previous experiences affect who and what we seek out in the world; therefore, the way we verbalise our thoughts and our reactions say more about our entire human experience than they do any one situation or thing. The purpose of understanding how we are neurologically and psychologically wired is so we can identify how human emotionality functions in players.

## Emotionality: Where Feelings Derive From

Emotion is the difference between a *reaction* and a *response*. We react in the hope of escaping potential danger, returning to the comfort of the known. The way we respond is unique to every individual; the way we react is not. A reaction is an overt response to unknown data with fear. A reaction manifests itself through verbal and nonverbal language and can clearly reveal player subjectivity. Human emotion can be simply deconstructed into an emotional dichotomy: love and fear. Every single feeling we experience is a derivative of one or the other emotional origin: love or fear.[8]

Here is how we interpret love and fear in a way that is relevant to our understanding of human behavioural and emotional trends.

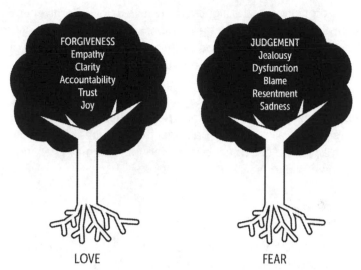

Diagram 13.3. Emotional dichotomy: love and fear

## Love

The many brands that have attempted to conceptualise its emotional nature have distorted our experience of love. When we think love, images of love hearts and Cupid, Valentine's Day and flowers, wedding dresses, and a particular person flood us. This is the modern-day brand of love. Accepting that love begins and ends with these mostly romantic concepts is to be subject to truths created by some other player who had an idea about love and was damn good at selling it.

Love is far more insightful and valuable to a human being. Anybody who shrugs off the power of love is simply afraid of it. Love is defined by the feelings that derive from it: empathy, compassion, and forgiveness, the epitome of creativity. These feelings affect the way we respond and behave to others. Choosing to approach the world with love awards us the ability to empathise and to forgive.

Forgiveness is the highest derivative of love. Forgiveness allows us to exist from an objective point of view. We understand that the way we receive people is a reflection of their previous experiences and the way we judge people is a reflection of ours.

Forgiveness allows us to empathise with those we encounter and understand their perspective. Understanding perspective allows us to gain insight and speak to people from a place of acceptance, even though they may challenge our own comforts.

## Fear

Fear has also been defined conceptually and associated with weakness or wimp-ish behaviour. We assert our ego in the face of fear, so others do not judge us in an attempt to appear strong. Fear is the guiding mechanism that keeps us within the known and comfortable. To live in fear is to allow resentment, jealousy, and hate with judgement as the highest derivative of fear.

Judgement is a reaction to the unknown. We judge what is different or unknown to us. We judge those who do or say things that compromise the comforts of our emotional territory. The body has a number of ways to respond to fear, and we have evolved past the point of fighting or running away from the things we do not know. We use feelings of fear to express how we really feel. We respond with anger and satire. We camouflage fear with unloving behaviour that is deemed acceptable in everyday society, judgement.

Essentially understanding our emotional foundations allows us to comprehend emotional outputs in the form of response and reaction, allowing us to objectify and map our own emotional territory and similarly map out those of other players. We are able to understand why we feel the way we do toward certain people and brands and similarly relate this knowledge to the behaviours and actions of others.

For a player seeking to influence players, this knowledge is gold in deciphering the emotional parameters of an intended niche market. As players, we can invoke empathy or loving behaviour into our insights' strategies to understand the subjective predisposition of a collective group or niche market.

A winning player understands that empathy creates opportunity much the same way fear senses it. In order for us to use empathy, we must come from a place of forgiveness, mindful of our own subjectivities and not defensive of (nonexistent) truths.

Empathy allows for the shift in power between players.

## How to Read Fear

If a player responds to us with anger, resentment, or judgement, this gives us the insight that something about us or who and what we represent is causing him or her to respond from a derivative of fear. Something about what we are saying, doing, or presenting is compromising their comfort zone and threatening their ego.

Often, our everyday experience of feelings like resentment, jealousy, and hate say more about us than they do about anybody or anything else. When we abide by man-made rules, we are naturally tempted to break them and therefore use judgement to commend obedience or to punish disobedience. We project judgement on others because we resent our own inability to break free from the rules. Resentment fuels jealousy and hate for people who seem unrestricted by these same rules.

This is why institutions built on fear set out to create it. Fear creates self-regulating humans who judge other humans based on man-made rules. The only winner in this equation is the inventor who profits from the rules.

## Both Love and Fear Are Equal in Their Power

How we perceive the world is how we will receive it. How we receive the world is thanks to how we perceive it. This notion is riddling, but this is a game, entrepreneur. It has its tricks and loopholes. It's exciting and dangerous at the same time. It requires us to use our brain.

If we perceive the game with forgiveness, we are empathetic to the players within it. We are receptive to and understanding of their opinions and beliefs. In turn, these same players perceive us as forgiving and trustworthy, tools in creating influence and shaping the way a player experiences our brand.

If we are judgemental, we are ruled out of the game and marginalised by our own subjectivities. We are blindsided by our wants and needs and not receptive to those of other players. This may have worked in the past, but the evolution of technology has seen to it that capitalism becomes more empathetic for the purpose of influence. Thank you, Steve Jobs!

Realizing love and fear at play is a matter of objectivity, that is, how consciously aware we are of our emotions and how emotions influence our decisions. Are we responding to the world, or are we reacting to it? Are we actively making decisions or passively accepting decisions made in the past, relative to our perceived state of normal? Are we consciously creating opportunity and allowing the formation of new response patterns, or are we subconsciously rejecting opportunities to stay comfortable? Is our gut feeling embracing opportunity or keeping us stagnant and safe?

The difference is a matter of playing the game or being played. The more we seek to understand the unknown, the less we fear it. The more we understand the reason behind why we judge, the easier it is to forgive.

For a winning player, fear is our greatest ally. The unknown and rush hormones attributed to fight-or-flight indicate that we are entering a world of opportunity.

## Chapter Fourteen

# THE BUSINESS OF PLAY

## The Business Lifecycle: What This Means for Us Entrepreneurs

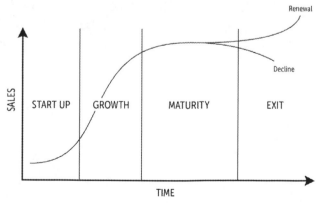

Diagram 14.1. The business lifecycle.

## Currency within the Game

Business is the exchange of object currency, money, or numbers indicating the profit and loss balance in a business. Branding is the exchange of subject currency, human influence, or exchange of an idea for human loyalty. Emotions navigate players through their decision-making process. The ability to emotionally affect another player results in brand advocacy.

An influential brand is one rich in subject currency. This brand has the power to leverage its influence when negotiating for object currency. Wealth comes from valuable brands.

Value is equal to the sum of all its parts: (Brand x Product) / Influence.

- Brand: an idea that speaks to a relevant market in a relevant way
- Product: a physical creation or productised service embodying the idea
- Influence: a brand's wealth in subject currency and its future potential for emotional engagement with a relevant market

# Branding: In the Schism of Things!

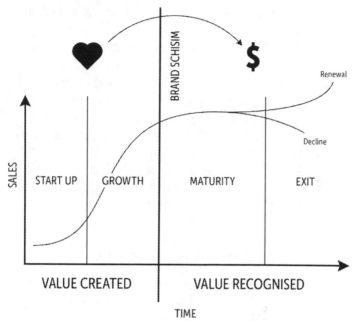

Diagram 14.2. The Brand Schism.

## The Brand Schism

The Brand Schism implies that there are two phases in business perspective relevant to determining the value of a brand. This pre- and post-schism phase assessment of the business lifecycle is relevant for achieving entrepreneurial perspective. At The Brand Schism, an entrepreneur can leverage their influence, subject currency, accrued in the pre-schism phases of business (start-up and growth) to seek out lucrative partnerships, brand endorsement, expansion, or calculation of value for a strong exit, in post-schism value recognition.

## Pre-Schism Operations: Value Created

This phase is when a business owner works to accrue wealth in subject currency. The pre-schism phase involves:

1. Visual Branding: Name, logo, website, social media, and all assets that help bring the brand idea to life
2. Position Branding: How well a brand communicates its values and how well it is characterised through personality and engagement
3. Productivity: Products and/or services provided by the company
4. Subject Currency: Social influence, online following, subscription databases, and consumer sentiment for the brand (future potential)

## Post-Schism Operations: Recognised Value

This phase of business assesses opportunities for growth, expansion, acquisition, or exit. Essentially, this is the phase where a business owner can leverage their pre-schism value and social wealth for object currency, money.

## Entrepreneurial Perspective

*Challenge*

Develop a brand that offers a product and/or service that caters to the needs of a particular niche market and conveys a strong message for the purpose of creating influence. Entrepreneur, the key to winning in the game is creating a valuable brand. The business lifecycle seems straightforward, right?

So why then do entrepreneurs fail so often? Perhaps it's because money is a far simpler concept to fathom than influence. We simplify one idea but remain confused about the other, which is bizarre because both currencies are calculated with the same formula:

Object Currency:
Brand + Engagement = Value (Money Exchange)

Subject Currency:
Idea + Experience = Meaning

Brand and Idea are synonymous.
Engagement and Experience are synonymous.
Money Exchange is determined by the value of Meaning
    derived from the brand.

If meaning and value are synonymous, it is then in the best interest of the brand owner to control their consumer's experience.

If we Google the definition of a product and a service, we'd see that service is "the action of helping or doing work for someone" and product is "an article or substance that is manufactured or refined for sale." A service requires we "do something" for someone. A product requires we "provide something refined for sale" to someone.

The difference is that a service drives consumers into a derivative of fear. Consumers judge their experience with subjectivity (derive meaning from fear), affecting the value of the service. Whereas, a product built on its niche's subjectivities speaks to that group from a derivative of love (comfort and acceptance), increasing its value.

The post-schism value of a brand is an appraisal of how engaged consumers are with that brand and how valuable they find their experience. A valuable brand must productise their service to refine, simplify, and conceptualise the brand offer for consumers. Productising an offer also ensures that a brand receives a positive value appraisal when negotiating for object currency in the post-schism phase of the business lifecycle. While players subconsciously seek complexity in their own lives, they consciously choose simple ideas to represent them.

Let there be no ambiguity as to what we do, how we do it, and why. Simplicity compliments a player. It means they get it, they understood it, they want it.

## Chapter Fifteen

# HOW INFLUENCE IS MEASURED

There is no questioning that people are open and honest about how they feel, what they think, and how they experience brands. We can sense when someone or something is not genuine.

I have come across a number of entrepreneurs who are ecstatic about launching their brands into the free world of social media. The reality is that we have every opportunity to achieve whatever it is we want to achieve, but remember that nothing is ever free. Social media is hard work!

Building a brand in a social platform can be a volatile situation. When people love a brand, they love it. When they hate it, they loathe it. Social media is just that, social. We have to think about the people we surround ourselves with, the people we like, and the people we cannot stand to be around. A brand exists much the same. There is nothing more irritating than a person who claims to know everything and has been everywhere or somebody who says one thing and then does another. Our brand must be about something! We must be about something! Before we wish to brand that something, we have to believe it and communicate it with clarity and conviction.

A brand must exist wholeheartedly for one message. Make it an insightful message. Find the people who share this conviction, and invite them to join your brand. This is how we experience the world in real time and in social media.

Strong messages are exclusive. Defining our brands before they are put out into the world is a necessity. People who love our brand message will fight for it. Focus on building a community and showing gratitude for the members of that community, those who fight for the brand and allow it to exist.

Social connection comes from two primary motivations:

- Fear of missing out (FOMO), where a brand accumulates followers because it promises to satisfy broad aspirational visions as a "brand to watch".
- Emotional transaction, the exchange of meaning for loyalty, because the brand represents a strong emotional sentiment.

Both require strong and identifiable messages.

In the game, perception is reality. Understanding how a niche group want to be perceived is a sure way to bridge the gap between our brand and their known predisposition. A brand must never be defined by its partnerships or endorsements. It must be focused on communicating an idea first and then a product or service. Remember that value (money exchange) is synonymous with meaning.

## Chapter Sixteen

# FAILURE EXPLAINED!

Steve Jobs said, "Creativity is just connecting things." [9] Great business is about seeking out how things connect.

Business is built on how players function. The game is built for human players by human players. This insinuates that a collective group of players understand humans better than humans understand themselves. All hail the 1 per cent!

Challenging the things we have been conditioned to accept as truth is the only way to adopt a winning state of mind. Question everything! There is no such thing as truth. There are only ideas and those players who are good at selling them. We are conditioned to believe that there exist ways of being when there is no such thing in reality.

Diagram 16.1. The elephant and the pole.

The elephant and the pole refers to the work of German philosopher Georg Wilhelm Friedrich Hegel. Hegelian philosophy refers to an "objective idealism,"[10] the self-conscious and metaphysical connection of the human spirit to a higher natural source. Hegel "disliked the irresponsibilities of individual 'freedoms' as much as the dehumanizing effect of the capitalist market."[11]

The notion of a dehumanizing affect is explored in the example of the elephant and the pole and paralleled with Michel Foucault's notion of biopower. A traveller passing by a great big elephant chained to a pole asks the elephant's caretaker, "How is it that such a large animal does not break free from that little pole when it could do so easily?"

The caretaker responds, "The elephant has been chained to that pole at that distance from a baby. When at first it tried to break away, it could not, as it was smaller, and so it learnt and still believes that it cannot, even though it could now easily."

The elephant is not unintelligent. It is not so different from its mammalian counterpart, the human. The example may be a wildly overt demonstration of conditioning practice, but is the example of the elephant and the pole so different from the human who believes and abides by truth? Was it not the truth, as proven through experience of that elephant, to think that it could not break away from that pole?

So why then do we cling to truth, rules, laws, religions, institutes, and ideologies as though they were not set up to condition the way we think in much the same way as that elephant? Is the wildly overt example of the elephant and the pole so far removed from our experience of reality?

In the mind of an entrepreneur, the player amongst players, truth should no longer map out the parameters for opportunity. Fear should no longer be attributed with threat or danger. Love and fear should no longer fit in the religious dichotomy of good and evil. Fear should be experienced purely as another emotion that drives us toward creating a valuable brand that is both relevant and influential. How we play or are played in the game is a matter of how well we understand our own humanity and, in turn, the humanity of others.

"The words coming out of your mouth say more about you than they do about me." Words are insightful. They are emotions materialised that for any one person willing to listen can reveal the workings behind every poker face. Actions always speak louder than words. The actions that work with or against words reveal a player's intention.

## Key Insight

"People only care about what they want!"[12] All players are playing to win. The winning player invites the other player to think that he or she has won. Winning the game is not about our ego. Winning is about playing our competitors ego.

The better we read human functions within ourselves, the better we become at reading them in others. This is the teaching of "Know Thyself." Reading and responding to the subjectivities of other players without the need to assert our own ego is called empathy. Empathy is the secret to being influential. An influential brand is a valuable brand. Without empathy, we will never possess the ability to obtain true and relevant emotional insights, which drive marketing strategy and idea generation.

A player's inability to make the connection between the real (nature) and imagined (nurture) results in the justification of unloving behaviour.

## Subjectivity Takes Away from Our Ability to Do, Create, and Innovate

If we are not conscious of judgement as a derivative of fear and protector of our subjectivities, then we react and often describe the experience with learnt attributes such as negativity or hate, bad, and evil. These things do not exist.

Consciousness is the ability to realise that these adjectives are taught representations of fear, the fear toward the unknown, instead of actually existing as negativity or evil. Love and fear exist as universal energy, that which metaphysically binds all living things: animals, nature, humans, and the universe. Our perception of good and evil is created through religious truth, serving only to institutionalise the way we think. Thank you Aristotle.

Judgement can just as easily be used to create great business and relationships as long as we are conscious that judgement stems from an innate source of fear. Identifying this and having an internal dialogue to understand where the fear or personal insecurity stems from is the key to making an informed decision. In business, judgement may stem from your own personal insecurity or unrelenting standards, feelings of failure, or entitlement. Either way, our words and actions may be counterproductive as we marginalise those around us to assert a truth about ourselves. There is no "I" in value, and no player will ever be influenced with unloving behaviour. Failure explained!

Failure among entrepreneurs is so common because we often attempt to create and innovate from a place of disconnect. We do not properly understand our humanity and therefore misinterpret our instincts, misperceive others' intentions, and react to business problems irrationally. We become subjective about objects and consequently see the game as complex and unpredictable, hard, and impossible.

We are responsible for everything good and bad that happens to us. We must simplify our beliefs to achieve a sense of clarity. We can never escape the ego, but we can read the ego in play.

## Chapter Seventeen

# K'NO'WLEDGE IS EVERYTHING!

Our ability to interpret human functionality makes us better players. How we perceive the game and all its players is a matter of objectivity.

All players navigate their game plan from their comfort zone. This is a subjective field shaped by childhood experiences, along with social, cultural, political, and religious beliefs, which come together to form an imagined territory. The parameters of this territory set a player's code of conduct. From it, a player projects their wants and needs into the game and plays in accordance with seeking them out.

An imagined territory creates a reality for the player, a known space where a player can exist within and measure themself against with a set of imagined rules and truths. We seek comfort in groups of like-minded players and situations that resemble or mimic the known.

An imagined territory is inviting to all brands and players, as long as they share common values. The uniting of like-minded players and brands creates culture and celebrates truth through rituals, such as tradition. Within this territory, we find localised or niche formations, bound by age and interest.

Niche markets are united by common subjectivities and sympathise with each other as they have similar patterns of reacting and responding. Niche markets are characterised by common "ways of being." They seek to endorse one another's status through similar brands and associations; therefore, they usually display patterns in buying, recreational interests, thoughts, and feelings around particular ideas. Niche markets are united by common enemies and exist within an illusion that sustains a level of emotional comfort.

Diagram 17.1. Imagined Territory.

## Understanding an Imagined Territory

A niche market exists within the realms of an imagined territory. Common 'Points of No' unite players within it. An imagined territory presents a number of insights into a niche market:

1. Emotional Territory: Political, religious, cultural, and experiential teachings mapping the parameters of acceptability. These parameters declare known and unknown regions that assert a response or reaction.
2. Territorial Truths: A player's code of conduct, values, and beliefs.
3. Territorial Narrative: Ideologies that define the niche, for example, white picket fence, American dream, or mateship, the ideas that guide aspirational wants and needs.
4. Points of No: Incursion markers between known and unknown regions to connect the parameters of the territory, marking player likes, dislikes, tolerance and defence, and so forth.

## Subjective Reason

This is the perspective of a player from inside his or her imagined territory.

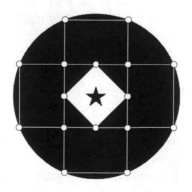

○ Point of No

Diagram 17.2. Subjective Reason: Points of No.

No is

- the centre of all judgement;
- clear mapping of known and unknown regions;
- defence of territorial truth, reinforcing territorial narrative and shaping perception;
- brands and organizations segmented according to similar or dissimilar values, upheld by the niche market to which an individual identifies with; and
- reaction points as a defensive mechanism to sustain comfort in the known and protect the illusion that a player imagines to be their reality.

## Points of No

This is the human emotional, psychological, and neurological reaction to an experience with a "No!" reaction. "No" is completely subjective, where reason is measured against territorial truths, forming the parameters of a players imagined territory. "No" similarly guides behavioural and consummatory patterns of a player.

In an imagined territory, players lack objectivity and are ruled by subjectivity in defence of their ego. This is the majority of the world's population. Every player exists within an imagined territory and either reacts or responds from it. The player who can understand this and draw out his or her own territory then has the power to read it in others. It becomes clear that we are never actually right or wrong. We are simply experiencing and perceiving the world according to our territorial truths and illusion of normality.

Arguing with another player is an attempt to assert our truths over theirs when both originate from imagined territories. This is the reality of every disagreement.

Speaking at a subjective player from a place of judgement is counterproductive to building an influential and valuable brand. Remember the brain is neurologically programmed to react to the unknown. Players will become defensive and perceive a threat when in the company of the unknown. Sensing this reaction should indicate to a winning player the need for empathy to find a common ground or value.

Marketing is the business of aligning one's brand with the territorial values of their niche market to establish a platform for engagement that invites their target market to imagine a new territory and grow together. A brand may offer an innovative solution to a niche problem, but if our brand message does not resonate with how that niche imagines their reality, then it is disregarded as unknown and irrelevant.

Remember, business is about building value. Value is influence. Influence is the ability to inspire an idea from within an imagined territory. This requires empathy, the ability to consciously backseat our own subjectivities and actively listen with an open and non-judgemental perspective. Imagined territories are invite-only. Players are only inviting if they sense us to be of the same imagined condition.

Ideas have no value if they cannot resonate with a particular group, who can give them life. Before picking an idea out of your wonderfully creative entrepreneurial mind, understand to whom this idea appeals to and why. Otherwise, we are simply creating art.

## Objective Reason

This is perspective outside of experience and the imagined territory.

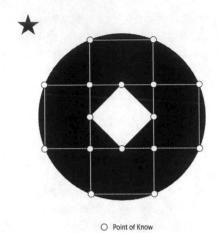

○ Point of Know

Diagram 17.3. Objective Reason: Points of Know.

## Points of Know

'Points of No' for a subjective player are 'Points of Know' for an objective player. Objective reason is the ability to understand experience met with a "No" reaction. For the purpose of influence, the player must avoid a "No" reaction or adapt their play strategy to accommodate a "No" reaction with a "Yes" response.

Entrepreneurial perspective is our ability to listen with objective reason and adapt to incoming (insightful) data with relevant responses. In other words, we must listen more than we speak. Respond to players, and never react to them. Objective reason gives players clarity. They can analyse the world with a fundamental understanding of how reason shapes behavioural patterns.

At the site where the known and unknown meet, are incursions that act as points of "No" or 'Know'. The difference is a matter of perspective. We are either confined by "No" or freed by being in the 'Know'.

Reason is understood by active observation. Human emotions and reactions reveal player subjectivity. Our ability to read these actions and listen for rejection cues will allow us to map out a player's imagined territory, which is seemingly representative of their entire niche.

The key strategy to playing the player and absolutely loving the game requires that we be present and truly engaged, we actively listen and respond, and we be empathetic.

Influence happens outside of the selling equation. Human engagement leaves a lasting impression on players. A player who inspires another with an idea becomes a selling machine. Remember that meaning is synonymous with money exchange. Humans do not buy products. They buy relationships and a sense of community. If our brand can invite and inspire people, then it is granted the love otherwise reserved for the people and brands within an imagined territory.

Hypothetically speaking, at no point am I ever willing to reveal myself, my needs, or my wants to somebody who seems disinterested or aloof to my personal experience. Trust requires equal emotional investment from opposing parties.

Without presence and active listening, we cannot possibly collect valuable human insights. Without insights, we cannot possibly determine what is relevant. Without relevance, we cannot possibly be engaging or memorable. Marketing is about drawing the connection between human psychology and human behaviour. It's all about what we 'know'.

Empathy is acknowledging a Point of No and responding to it without judgement.

## Chapter Eighteen

# A BRAND-NEW WORLD

Let's apply the things we've read about to analyse the market and build a truly relevant and engaging brand.

A brand is an idea that creates a new imagined territory. This territory is materialised through products and experiences. Seeding an idea into a niche market requires our brand share common values with it. Ideas fundamentally grow from the inside out and not typically from the outside in.

A brand with cross-territorial influence (appeals to more than one niche market) has the opportunity to create a whole new platform altogether as long as we can determine common territorial values across markets and convey these values in our marketing messages.

Entrepreneur, creativity and innovation is not a matter of reinventing the wheel. By all means, have a crack at it once you're a millionaire, but in the interim, focus on a lean start-up built on solid insights, remembering one key insight that humans fundamentally do not like change. They love their comfort zone. While we are the crazy ones and love the rush of the unknown, the great majority of the world is happy living in their normal.

Our ability to understand their territory and create something that is relevant and engaging is far more innovative than some foreign contraption that is unfamiliar and difficult to comprehend. This will make players feel stupid, a feeling they will happily project onto your amazing invention. The next thing you know, your stupid contraption is trending on twitter #fail.

A brand built on strong insights is one that is engaging, relevant, and simple to comprehend, primarily key aspects of a valuable brand. A brand written into a territorial narrative can affect more change than one that attempts to rewrite it all together. If our brand can engage a group of people, it is relevant. Relevance is the key to a hugely influential and valuable brand.

As entrepreneurs, we must remind ourselves that we are ultimately selling to humans. We too are human; therefore, we too are subject to our own territorial truths and emotional parameters. Understanding how humanity has come to function begins first with understanding how we function individually, "Know Thyself." The world is merely a projection of our own humanity.

Understanding how a niche market wishes to be perceived or wish to see themselves means we can tie elements of that façade into our marketing strategy and our brands vision.

## Chapter Nineteen

# GAME FACE

Creating a brand is a task that first and foremost requires a market. In business, if an idea is not relevant to anybody, then it is not creative. The demand for a solution should exist before we have invested time and money into creating it and trying to sell it. What is the unique offer? What gives the brand an exciting selling point? Where is the creativity in the brand, the sweet spot that resonates with a particular group of people?

A brand story requires a simple idea, built on a simple insight that inspires a market to dream and incites a want to buy. Simplicity is the understanding that humans seek complexity. Human insights come from understanding our market's complexities: their fears, values, Points of No, and aspirations. If winning is the business of keeping things simple, then building a brand is the business of understanding why players are so complex and speaking to this complexity with a simple solution that inspires how they see the world.

There is nothing more binding in the human experience than the feeling of being heard and the calm of finding a solution to a problem.


## Case Study: Nike "Just Do It"

Dan Wieden of Wieden + Kennedy was the man who came up with Nike's 1988 "Just Do It" slogan. In a 2009 *Adweek* interview at the twenty-fifth birthday of the Nike "Just Do It" ad campaign, Dan recounts how he came to those three words that now stand as one of the most successful slogans of our time. The night before the presentation to Nike in 1988, Dan was fretting that the strategy for the then twenty-five million-dollar campaign "wasn't hanging together" and feared that there was no standout message to unite all the different ideas and directors in such a broad marketing campaign.

Dan Wieden said, "Nike required a message that would speak to women who had just started walking to get in shape and people who were world-class athletes." He goes on to recall the trial of Gary Gilmore, a man who had been sentenced to death by firing squad after having committed murder in the state of Utah. When asked if he had any last words, Gary replied, "Yeah, let's do it." Dan understood the simplicity of this statement to be the key human insight when facing up to a challenge against your own will, uncertain of how much you want it, yet still with a mentality to just push through. This is the essence of having to suck it up against all odds and "just do it!"

Dan Wieden described coming to this insight as a simple thing and goes on to say, "Simplicity is really the secret of all big ideas." Insights are a "good peak into the subconscious and where ideas come from" (Dan Wieden 2009).

Understanding the human condition in its simplest form creates distinct roles for certain players, that of the conscious observer who can detect subconscious motivations and that of the subconscious player who is driven by their motivations. One player is selling; the other is buying.

As entrepreneurs, we pride ourselves on passion, the relentless pursuit of something we believe in, but we must keep things in perspective. Business is about building valuable brands for achieving a level of financial freedom. Entrepreneurial perspective is about emotional and professional objectivity. Professional objectivity is the understanding that we are not our brands. We are merely the CEOs employed to keep them functioning profitably in business. We can never be so subjective to believe that we are small enough to be defined by one particular brand or title. We are humans always open to opportunity.

The key to winning the game is to play with the intention to sell. We must learn to work with intention.

1. Build a brand within the emotional parameters of a sizeable niche market(s) because sizeable markets ensure sizeable reach.
2. Marry up market and brand values so the brand is relevant and has a platform for engagement.
3. Seek out existing big brands that share these same core values to leverage pre-schism value for endorsement, partnership, diversification, or exit.
4. Invite conversations that inspire thought, allowing players to associate the brand with bigger ideas.

The key to creating a valuable brand is to build it with the intention to sell it (exit strategy). This creates the type of mindset that is directive and concise when making decisions,

"Does this decision fit in with the brand vision? Does it add value at the finish line?"

Work with the intention to sell. Always!

## Build a Brand with the Exit Strategy in Mind!

For a brand to be attractive to buyers, it must embody four key qualities:

1. Vision: imagined territory
2. Values: emotional parameters of this territory
3. Personality: central message
4. Positioning: unique selling point

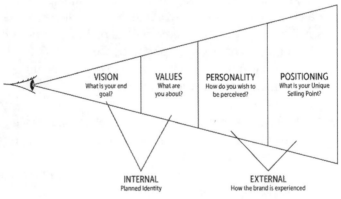

Diagram 19.1. Brand projection.

## Vision

A brand must have an origin (insight) and a destination (solution). A brand vision is an idea. Part of selling an idea is inspiring consumers to own it. Inspire players to imagine themselves as part of it. A brand creates a platform for what could be or what could happen. It is selling this type of opportunity that generates brand advocacy. Players are always fantasizing about the opportunities that lie in an ideal world. If we can understand these fantasies, we can offer a brand that alludes to their appeal.

For example, the Apple brand is about creating the future of tomorrow, that is, endless possibility. Apple sells this vision by supplying the products to achieve it. The Apple brand creates the opportunity for us to turn dreams into a reality and is therefore experienced as an empowering brand, one that reminds us to "Stay hungry. Stay foolish." Empowerment, innovation, creativity, and freedom are the values at the core of the Apple brand and are used to express Apple's vision. The infamous 1984 Apple ad directed by Ridley Scott, a director made famous by his futuristic film *Blade Runner* (1982), was about breaking free from the establishment, escaping from those responsible for stealing our ideas and our dreams. The nonconformist, the individual, fighting for freedom, chasing opportunity with Apple by their side. The human computer, against the robot human. This type of vision made us fall in love with Apple.

## Values

A brand must be built on a set of core values. Strong insights drive marketing strategy, product development, and partnerships. The better we understand the values and truths of our niche market, the more we can incite a want to buy. Brand values outline the emotional parameters, dos and don'ts, truths, and aspirations of the brand.

A strong set of brand values will fundamentally align our brand with a particular niche market and existing big brands. How well we express these values in our branding will determine future opportunities in the post-schism phase.

For example, Nespresso coffee brand targets a sophisticated coffee connoisseur. Their values are sophistication, classic design, and quality. These core values instruct product design, retail engagement, and marketing strategy. One key brand ambassador for Nespresso is actor George Clooney, who exists as an extension of these brand values, a similarly classic, sophisticated ambassador for the brand. It is important to note that George Clooney is also aligned with fashion brand Armani. This is a strategic value adding partnership, whereby Nespresso extends its brand into the realm of luxury and prestige, sophistication, and classic design through partnership.

Branding is never about selling products. It's always about selling community. Players want to be part of the cool kids in their niche market. The way they express their coolness is by celebrating the values that unite them. Understanding brand values is vital for relevant product development and marketing strategy.

## Brand Personality

What is your brand story? Define a lead protagonist. How has the brand come to exist? What problem does it solve? How do you see your brand? Why is your brand relevant? These questions shape our brand personality. If our brand were a person, how would he or she dress? How would he or she speak? Where would he or she shop? What would he or she do recreationally? Is our brand a he or a she?

Humans don't fall in love with brands. They fall in love with how brands make them feel. If our brand can adopt human characteristics, then it is more likely to resonate with a human market. This is why brand endorsement is so successful. People want to associate with people. If they have the opportunity to buy fame or luxury, practicality, or authority through association with a product or service, then they will.

We must answer how we want our brand to make people feel. Does this feeling stem from love or fear? Understanding the emotional derivatives of our brand also guides our marketing strategy.

For example, certain pharmaceutical brands use fear to promote their products. They enlist doctors and specialists to endorse their brands and authenticate their clinical value. They use fear to assert necessity and importance. Luxury brands also use fear and judgement in their marketing campaigns to invoke a fear of missing out, the party you weren't at, or the clothes you can't afford. This type of emotional strategizing creates a need for purchase. Our ego wants to be realised in alignment with a particular value, for example, luxury, it will set out to fulfil a sense of belonging. Alternatively, food brands use love—family, dinner table, holiday gatherings, and celebration of the comfort zone—to evoke a sense of warmth and appetite.

Players want to be a part of a story. They want something to believe in, a hero and an idea.

## Brand Positioning

What is it about our brand that makes it unique or special? A unique selling point is our brand edge. What makes us so spunky? Coming to realise our brand uniqueness is not always about kicking up a media storm. If our brand delivers its core values exceptionally well in a marketplace where competing brands are mediocre, then it is unique. A unique selling point is very much dependent on how well we understand our niche market and their influences. Think relevance!

Here's something to consider. Brand direction comes from how well we understand the wants and needs of our intended market. Innovation comes from how well engaged we are with this market. Now, more than ever, brands need to invite their consumers to contribute to how they exist and ask for direction.

The current media landscape demands brands build genuine relationships in order for them to survive. It is necessary that we understand our relationships with consumers to mimic those relationships we have with our friends. Consumers and brands are so tightly intertwined in each other's lives that it would seem a missed opportunity if we did not invite them in to help us develop our brand position.

Winning brands are those built for the people and by the people, hence the explosion of crowdsourcing, people collaborating to create. When we invite people and their ideas to contribute to our brand, they feel a sense of ownership and protection over the brand they helped create. Relationships are all about emotional investment. We need to embrace the free tools of social media for creative direction and in building a community.

This is very much the current marketing strategy employed across a number of industries. The music industry has used this type of marketing to build an edge into their artist brands. Artists like Lady Gaga invite fans to explore her brand through branded content campaigns, like Art Pop extending the Gaga brand far beyond the realms of music and promoting brand engagement. On the other hand, artists like Lana Del Rey completely changed the way the music industry does business. Her approach to the music industry was entrepreneurial and pure business romance. She established herself as an independent artist who sought out to create a fan base organically through social media. Lana Del Rey is more than just a pretty brand. She speaks to the melancholy that is teenage adversity and made herself a presence in relevant social media channels, like Tumblr. Lana Del Rey used social media to build influence in what was a strong pre-schism strategy and then used her influence to negotiate her contractual agreements with not one but a number of recording labels in the post-schism conversion of value for money. This is an example of how creating a solid pre-schism brand strategy can be leveraged for post-schism negotiation of object currency.

## Chapter Twenty

# PLAYERS ONLY KNOW GOOD STORIES

Players believe in brands that affect them emotionally. This is why good stories are told and retold. Humans are united by common enemies and, more often than not, celebrate heroes that embody their common values. This is the foundation for understanding why certain ideas resonate with particular groups of like-minded players. We have come to understand the world in binaries, known and unknown, good and evil, and hero and villain. Binaries create the need for advocacy as we are either for or against.

Storytelling is the foundation of everything we know. It is the format for how we recall experiences, recount events, and declare notions of self. The biggest brands in the world, from Coca-Cola to McDonald's and Apple, are fundamentally built on stories that follow the same plot. In 2013, the BBC released a three-part documentary titled *Secrets of the*

*Super Brands* with Alex Riley. The documentary used MRI screening tests to observe human response patterns to super brands such as Apple and uncovered that brands "have harnessed or exploit the brain areas that have evolved to process religion."

The documentary goes on to parallel the common denominators between religion and super brands, describing brands as having adopted the same format of storytelling, hero revival and worship, as the major religions of the world.

At the core of both big brands and big religions are great stories with leading good heroes such as the Messiah and Steve Jobs with similar tales of their apocalyptic battles and struggles in overcoming adversity, the devil, and IBM. Alex Riley goes on to compare similarities in the way we experience these brands, the church, and the Apple store as a place of worship and, of course, the symbols at the centre of their brand, the crucifix and the Apple logo.

We have become accustomed to a traditional style of storytelling, and to some extent, we seek out the stereotypes. It is satisfying to know that the good guy will win and the bad guy will lose. As entrepreneurs, we want to be creative, and we want to challenge norms and be innovative. But this is a challenge that the majority of players are not willing to take. For our brands to survive the start-up, we must utilise the comfort of tradition and well-tested models to tell our story and communicate our ideas.

Incorporating traditional storytelling into our brand is the first step to being positively received by its market. It is the format for fairy tales, religious doctrine, films, and entertainment that have conditioned us to expect certain outcomes and characterizations. A good leading protagonist who overcomes adversity and defeats a villainous bad guy is a story that excites the comforts of our known territories. An emotional message or key sentiment invites the consumer on a journey with the brand.

Be reminded that business is fundamentally the art of selling to humans. We, humans, only ever care about what we want. Players are more than willing to invest in a brand that has invested time into understanding their wants and needs to create an offer that is simple and relatable.

## Chapter Twenty-One

# THE OFFER

Simplicity is genius. Complexity is fear. Business is explaining in simple terms what we do, why, and for whom. Simple.

A complex answer will confuse and offend players. If our brand confuses people, it makes them feel defective and stupid, "Is it me or …" The thought alone insults the ego, and our brand is now associated with feelings of stupidity and defectiveness. Players will not personalise these feelings as easily as they will project them onto our brand. In turn, they will avoid our brand and us so they do not feel this way again.

A complex explanation also insinuates that we cannot commit to doing one thing brilliantly. Players who ramble are perceived as untrustworthy. How can we possibly deliver solutions when we don't clearly understand the problem, cannot communicate the obstacles, and have no vision?

Simplicity makes a player feel great about themselves. He or she actually understands our ideas, and our brand is now associated with positive reward. The emotional integrity of our story affects the way it is perceived. When we go to the cinema to watch a film, the minute that movie is finished, we are quick to pass judgement. The film was either good or crap. We either recommend it to our friends or tell them not to bother. Buying the DVD or watching the sequel completely depends on the story and the execution at first go.

It is important that we understand our brand and apply its message three-dimensionally. We must embrace our consumers' perspective and judge our brand objectively from their points of view. How would they see this brand? This is where we need to understand the difference when selling a product or service and the impact each offer has on brand experience.

## Productizing Our Approach to the Game

Cinemas make money because they have productised the cinematic experience. We purchase the tickets first and then watch the movie. They realise that, if people had the option of paying after they had watched the movie, some might say the fee was unjustifiable, as the movie was rubbish (in their opinion). Why then do entrepreneurs and business owners put themselves in these same situations? It's suicide!

If we wish to make money in business, we must simplify our offer and the way in which our brand is received. We need to be in the business of delivering one big idea at a time, simple and relatable. Simplicity does not allow the mind to drift or become overwhelmed with options. Entrepreneur, productise everything you offer. Consumers respond positively to simplicity. Complex offers and ideas create unease and can assert all sorts of feelings that unfortunately seem to always find themselves free styling across the Twitterverse.

While the experience of both a product and service equally affects the branding or experiential aspect of a brand in the same way, we must do everything in our power to own the information and control the consumer experience to a certain degree. Consumers take to the marketplace with conviction. They say, "I know my rights." When purchasing a product, they pay first and use later. When purchasing a service, they use first and pay later. The difference is that, for as long as there has not been any exchange of money, the consumer has the power to negotiate value.

This is what a service means for a consumer. Consumers will without a doubt exercise their power and their negotiation skills to get the best possible deal. It isn't because they need it. It's because we gave them the option to do so. Consumers will exercise their power to negotiate price as they weigh up the quality of the service to the price of it and will almost always seek out a customised version of the service with the understanding that a service provider needs to impress them in order to secure a sale.

This is what service means for a business. Service means that the business must put up the time and cost of producing its offer before it exchanges money for it. This means the business works in a negative cash flow[13] as it must fund the service and sale before seeing any form of income. A service impacts brand experience, as repeat purchase is subject to the personal relationship established between the service provider and the consumer.

Productizing creates a positive cash flow into the business.[14] With a product, the consumer has learnt to pay first and use later. It takes away the consumers' right to negotiate and customise, but more importantly, it requires the consumer to engage with the brand direct, that is, the information provided through the packaging, price point, advertising material, and public profile rather than one single disinterested sales assistant, or a tired and stressed out business owner.

When a consumer engages with a product brand, the brand-owner possesses the power to control what is seen and a consumer's exposure to information. As entrepreneurs, our understanding of our niche market should mean that our product speaks to their core values and appeals to their perception of self.

Productizing is a way of isolating brand engagement to one's experience of a product, eliminating the brand owner and retail experience from the equation. We need to focus on creating brands that have character and isolate brand experience to an imagined platform (packaging, advertising, social media, and website). The brand message must resonate with its intended market. The romance must exist outside of the buying equation.

Remember, consumer and brand engagement mimic the way we engage in social circles. Like friends, our products exist as an extension of our own personality or perceived sense of self. Brands must invite consumers into their imagined world in a way that a consumer feels the brand is a representation of them and an extension of self.

## Chapter Twenty-Two

# GREAT GAME

### Alexander the Great

'Alexander' the Brand was brought to life by a leading hero that Alexander himself envisioned and set out to create. Alexander embodied the mythological allure of the Hellenistic period that saw him rise to the title of son of Zeus. Of course, this title was more rumour than fact, but it was enough to seed his brand as a divine military conqueror, a human of greater ability. Alexander understood the concept of branding in that perception is reality and, in turn, set out to shape the perception of himself as the son of Zeus, claiming further endorsement of his title by the Oracle. The thing about rumours in a contextually superstitious day and age is that no body of people would dare question the divinity of a man rumoured to be a god, out of fear of his wrath.

There is no doubt that this Hellenistic warrior was great, but was it his divinity or his brilliantly strategic mind that led him to conquer half the globe? Was Alexander the greatest entrepreneur of his time?

Alexander did not rely on his military regime to enforce Hellenistic doctrine or truth. Instead, he was receptive to the people and cultures he came across, conforming to their ways of thinking and allowing himself to experience their beliefs and traditions without judgement. This is what made Alexander great! His brand was infused into every culture that he encountered. When he conquered Egypt, he became a Pharaoh, Zeus Amun. Alexander the Great used empathy to play through his own ego into the hearts and cultures of newfound people, showing them how he was similar. Alexander never highlighted his difference. He only ever set out to draw attention to their common values. This made him influential and still a relevant case study for today.

Greatness comes from understanding one fundamental truth about human desire, that is, "Humans only care for what they want."[15] If we approach a group of like-minded people pushing opposing truths and beliefs, opposition would meet us. Setting aside judgement of otherwise unknown traditions and cultures invites empathy. Embracing difference from a place of intrigue paves the path for influence. Our intention in business is to build a valuable brand. Building a brand requires vision; creating value requires influence.

## Strategic Thinking

### The Formula: Vision - Obstacle = Strategy

Entrepreneur, have a vision of success, a desired position in the world. This involves the greatest strength and power of mind in overcoming insecurity and even the doubts presented with opportunity. The fear of overcoming the unknown is no simple task. A strategy is the difference between a dream and a goal. Business is about the exchange of subject currency for object currency, human influence for money. We need to seek and create value out of everything and everyone we come across. This is what it means to be an entrepreneur. There is no such thing as wasted time or lack of opportunity. Opportunity is the essence of business, presenting itself to any one person willing to see it. We cannot see it without wanting to.

Playing to win requires that we establish a winning vision. Reaching that vision is a matter of identifying the obstacles currently stopping us from getting to it. Overcoming obstacles requires clarity, a mindset that says, "I can and will because somewhere somehow there is a solution to dissolve this obstacle."

Success has nothing to do with dreaming, wishing, or hoping. But if dreaming, wishing, and hoping are meditative tools to sustain a level of objectivity and a sense of clarity, then dreaming, wishing, and hoping are a necessity.

Entrepreneur, let's do what we do, think strategy!

- Vision: We are the masters of our own business empire.
- Obstacle: Humans are so self-consumed. How do we get them to love our products?
- Strategy: Pick one niche market. Research this market. Identify where they are at what time, how they speak, and with whom. What they want? Why? Seek to understand what is relevant to them. Create a community that supports your brand because your message says something about who they are as a collective.
- Understanding the nature of human emotionality is the secret to knowing that human better than they know themself. Loving responses represent known comfort, and reactions represent fear

of the unknown. In order to engage with a niche market, we must engage within its known comfort. Understanding what the known holds to be true reveals insights into that player's wants, needs, and aspirations. Play the player. Love the game!

We cannot sell an idea, product, or service from a Point of No. At a Point of No, we get no-thing: no connection, no influence, no advocacy, and no word of mouth. Our pitch may be perfect, but it is falling upon deaf ears because our message is not relevant.

Irrelevance breeds dysfunctional thinking. This is precisely the type of thinking we must seek clarity to avoid. This type of dysfunctionality ignites personal insecurity in us. We begin to evaluate our abilities and talents when really we just haven't done enough research.

Clarity and objectivity, forgiveness, and non-judgement allow us to hear an opportunity when it presents itself. Listen for opportunity. Be present and empathetic, engage with humans, and seek to embrace their oddities because business is ultimately the art of selling to humans.

A good conversation is more valuable to branding than money or gold because it builds trust. Trust is the emotional bond created between two people that connect in a loving and empathetic way. This is the epitome of positive brand engagement. Trust creates the foundation for solid influence. An influential brand is a valuable brand. Trust is the difference between perceived positive and negative gut feelings.

Listen and respond. Players will love you for it!

## Chapter Twenty-Three

# THE GREAT STRATEGY

Entrepreneur, sit down, shut up, stop talking, stop selling, stop trying to convert. And listen. Great business comes from great understanding! The words that come out of your mouth say more about you than they do about me. (It's repeated here for effect.) Decipher the wants and needs of a niche market by asking questions. Listening and observing are tools used by winning players for understanding context.

I recall the first entrepreneur I ever pitched, for a potential partnership. I get nervous even thinking back to that day. I had moved to Europe to work on a project in the music industry. He was exactly the person I was looking for and I remember going into his office and talking nonstop for an hour. I had an answer for every question, and I had an idea for every suggestion. I was playing the worst kind of game, constantly waiting for my turn to speak. I had this fire in me that I needed to bring out. I needed to prove the things I knew and convince him that I was on to something.

At the end of the meeting, he said he would be in touch. I remember crying all the way home. I was exhausted and scared. Here I was, twenty-four years old in a foreign country, having invested all my money into one idea, one that meant the world to me. I replayed the conversation over and over in my head, so much so I have completely distorted the memory of that day. I still can't recall it properly.

Finally after two days of feeling hysterical, he called, wanting to set up another meeting. In my completely subjective state, I heard the fight bell go off. Ding ding! Round two! I made up another awesome PowerPoint presentation, building on the ideas I had talked about in the first meeting. And boy, did I let him have it. Looking back now, I get this visual of me bashing that poor man over the head with my laptop, screaming ideas at him and dancing around like that scene from the film *Jerry Maguire* (1996). "Show me the money!" I was out of my mind, crazy and delusional.

Imagine what he was thinking. I left that meeting feeling uncomfortable. Again, it remains a blur. But he called again. This time round, I was kind of exhausted. I recall there being a lot of talking and laughing in the previous meetings, but still no offer on the table. Still, there was no solid direction. I sat more reserved in that third meeting, I had practically talked myself silent. He noticed the change in me and laughed.

"What happened?" he blurted out with a laugh that made his belly bounce.

He was a big guy, almost as tall as me, six-foot-two, full-figured, and tanned with a dark beard.

He said, "What do you want to do?"

My heart sank. I thought to myself, *Honestly, I have talked relentlessly, and yet, I still cannot tell him in one sentence what I want, and it's obvious he doesn't actually know what to give me.*

I felt defeated, and he could see it. It wasn't until I finally shut up and let him speak that I leant something. Actually, I learnt a whole lot. Those three months changed my entire life. I never had him as a mentor, but his words were like gold. The more I listened, the richer I got. He taught me the power of listening.

As players in the game, we are either playing or being played. In trying to impress him, I told him everything I knew and every idea I had ever conceived. It was so satisfying to my ego to parade around my brilliant ideas. As a wiser man, he just listened quietly, and he knew how to shut me up. Ask for something simple! At the time, I felt like I was the winning player. In reality, I was playing in his game. He let me think I had called the shots, but he was writing the rules.

## Play Action

Listen and respond. Nothing destroys presence more than waiting idle for your turn to speak. Listen for responses and reactions. Ask questions to decipher one's vision, and seek to understand the obstacles preventing that vision from coming into fruition. Strive to become a part of the solution. This is the secret to selling.

## Build a Brand around Relevance

Active listening will reveal every sales strategy you need to engage your niche market. Active listening will allow you to map out a player's imagined territory. People love talking about themselves. In fact, they are very open about their Points of No. We often hear people say, "No, I would never do that … That is just so unacceptable … OMG!"

## Task

The next time you have a conversation with somebody, listen for his or her Points of No and ask questions about them and what they like or dislike and why. Attempt to mentally construct the emotional parameters around that person. Ask questions that invite responses, genuinely listen, and respond to that person. It might be surprising how taken aback they are by your intrigue.

As an experiment, establish a common ground with that person and build ideas off it. See what opportunities the two of you can create out of nothing. This type of engagement invites harmony, creativity, and innovation.

In a world where our personal brand is the only thing that differentiates us from one another, then our sole purpose should be not to compete but to inspire. Inspiring others to dream up ideas is our ability to influence creativity. Our ability to do so results in our personal brand being associated with positivity and inspiration.

## What's Yours Is Mine, What's Mine Is Yours, LOL Jokes, Is Mine!

Humans are emotional about ownership. Ownership is the ego trying to define itself in material form. Invite players to contribute to your ideas and your inventions. This is a great way to build relationships, create brand endorsement, and stage your brand for relevant strategic partnerships. Collaboration among players helps to build a brand organically. Players involved in building the brand will feel a sense of ownership over it, a brand they help create. Ownership promotes positive endorsement.

## Tools for Understanding Consumer Relevance and Becoming Influential

Creating an influential brand requires building a brand in a hungry territory, whereby there is an appetite for it. How can we satisfy somebody's appetite when we have no idea what he or she craves?

- Be empathetic and forgiving. Listen for and respond to Points of No without judgement.
- Give the player a feeling of importance by being present in the conversation. Presence is more engaging than any sales pitch. "We are interested in others when they are interested in us."[16]
- Invite players to be a part of your ideas, promote suggestions, and seek out their advice. They are enormous advocates of their own ideas.
- Have gratitude. We are in the business of selling to humans. Set out to create real relationships. Consider the "Emotion In: Logic Out" ratio. Profit and loss is relative to the level of engagement we bring to a conversation.
- Replace fear with exhilaration. Anything and anyone we aspire to be exists in the realms of the unknown. The unknown is opportunity. Players who are different to us exist in the unknown. They too are opportunity.
- For entrepreneurial perspective, do not get defensive about truth. Everything we know to be real and true was made up by a man or woman, no more or less capable than you or I who had an idea and was damn good at selling it.
- Entrepreneur, nothing exists. You choose!

## Chapter Twenty-Four

# PHILOSOPHY BEHIND THE WIN

A shift in perspective is rather simple to theorise about. It is relatively easy to imagine that we exist and experience the world perched on a branch belonging to either a tree of love or fear, objectively or subjectively, but it is crucial to understand the self from an original state of being, a natural state as opposed to the way we have become, a nurtured state. Aristotle asserted the concept of metaphysics and explored an *Arche* or origin of existence from one universal source of energy that connects all living things to each other.

Entrepreneur, winning in the game almost entirely relies on our ability to consciously challenge everything we know and seek out the unknown. Understanding that every complexity surrounding us is a construct built on fear allows us to assess institutions and institutional ways of thinking and the way that logic has come to shape truth. Creativity and innovation comes from freeing oneself of truth.

Nothing inspires humans more than nature. Nature is the ego's greatest threat, as it cannot be defined or measured by a name. Nature is not spoken about. It is felt. Perhaps it is our natural ability to inspire that gives us power in the game.

What is the difference between somebody who inspires us and somebody who bores us half to death? What is the difference between a presentation that motivates us to want something and one that struggles to keep us awake? Is it the use of words or actions? I think not. Both kinds of people ultimately use words and actions. Is it the delivery? The way we perform? Our enthusiasm that inspires people to do? Perhaps, but then again, there is nothing less convincing than a disingenuous show.

What is it about being genuine that incites a want to buy? There are no words or actions to endorse genuine feelings. There is only the feeling of being genuine that is exchanged between players. In other words, selling is the exchange of feelings, affections that derive from emotionality projected away from and to the human body through vibrational energy.

Further inquiry into the mammalian species reveals that we have a natural ability to communicate using energy sound waves and vibrational energy. There is a lot to be said for the nonverbal exchange of meaning that we use in our everyday experience of business. Human beings only see one part of the electromagnetic spectrum that surrounds us, visible light. Does this mean that, because we do not see the remaining radio, microwave, infrared, ultraviolet, x-ray, and gamma rays, they do not exist?

An entire reality exists outside of our perception. Animals are the best example of this. Elephants communicate to each other using infrasound waves[17] ranging between fourteen and twenty-four hertz at a volume between eighty-five and ninety decibels. Humans hear sound in the range of twenty to twenty thousand hertz, generating conversations at around sixty-five decibels.[18] Therefore, we are unable to hear elephants communicate. Similarly, rats communicate through vibrational energy called vocalizations. When seeking or courting sexual partners, they do so at a vibrational frequency level of fifty KHz. They are able to shift their frequency levels to communicate different feelings, for example, twenty-two KHz vocalizations indicate resting patterns and post-intercourse downtime.[19] We must be conscious of the energy that we cannot see. Just because we cannot hear elephant infrasound waves or feel rat vocalizations, should not discount from the fact that these modes of communications exist within our species.

There is a very real notion at play here in that humans also possess the ability to conduct vibrational energy in a way that affects behaviour nonverbally. Have you ever sat down next to somebody who was upset and sensed how he or she was feeling? Have you ever walked away from an amazing conversation and felt as though you were flying? Do we not sense tension amongst friends? How do we know when to trust people or empathise with them?

Aristotle said, "All men by nature seek to know."[20] This begs the question: Have we lost our desire to seek out what is natural? Or is the material world so distracting that we choose not to actually know anything? If we have lost our natural want to seek out knowledge, then does that mean we have also lost our humanity?

The game and all its players has become so dependent on brands that we have no idea how to define ourselves outside of them, so we build our entire identity, tradition, and culture around ideas and claim them as truth. We liken truth to nature and draw up rules enforcing this truth on the pretence of nature. Our ego is so defined by the material world that it begs the question: Are we not robotic imitators of the human kind? Have we so regulated the way we use emotion that love is reserved for comfort and fear is attributed to all things unknown? Do we manipulate our natural powers to suit the world we live in, much the same way we manipulate the natural environment to support the material world we've built?

Let's consider breaking all the rules. Imagine the possibility of taking to the unknown with love and an awareness of our nurtured state of fear. No thing would intimidate us.

Is this not how we glorify successful entrepreneurs today? Richard Branson comes to mind. The world seems content to rationalise his level of crazy against his wealth as somewhat of an anomaly. What is up for consideration here is not Richard Branson's wealth. It is the mindset that seemingly got him that wealth that should interest a young entrepreneur. There is something wild and untamed about that man: a fire in his eyes, a seemingly carefree and forgiving attitude, and a relentless pursuit to win. From afar, I'd describe him as fun and funny, unpredictable, and intimidating all at the same time. Sure, this is the pretence of his personal and professional brand, but Richard Branson seems to genuinely endorse these attributes. So his madness is believable and likeable. His brand appears natural, so he is captivating.

This kind of winning player sees the world differently. Their point of view affects the way they perceive and receive the world and, in turn, affects the way they are perceived and received by the world. This binary of understanding is completely attributed to vibrational energy.

For example, consider the energy field of a human in a city.

Diagram 24.1. Subjective point of view.

## Projecting Weak Vibration

The enormity and overwhelming weight of the material world is crushing the player. They perceive money, brands, bricks, and steel to hold value and are therefore marginalised by their ego. The subjective player receives the world in the hierarchy that they perceive it with them at the bottom.

Diagram 24.2. Objective point of view.

## Projecting Strong Vibration

The player is conscious of their metaphysical connection to all things natural. The city is nothing but bricks and steel bound together by humans, no more or less capable than they are. The material world sits idle. It has no energy. It is a material wasteland compared to the universal power that they have access to. The natural world ignites every element within them and they embrace living energy amongst powerless objects.

Entrepreneurialism is the initial struggle between the old and new. It is the conflict that one player endures in coming to terms with nature and nurture and the struggle to gain perspective. This is the process known as being entrepreneurial. Good business is just a clear understanding and an application of appraisal systems. Socrates said, "The secret of change is to focus all of your energy, not on fighting the old, but on building the new." [21]

Entrepreneurialism requires the abandonment of old values for new, usually requiring us to break up with unloving people and unloving situations that create dysfunction. I call these unloving people "freaks of nurture." Seek out the "freaks of nature". They have drifted from the old and are insightful. Conversations with these people are inspiring and creative!

## Chapter Twenty-Five

# THE PLAYER AMONGST PLAYERS

In the playbook of every entrepreneur, there should be outlined the strategy for satisfying one fundamentally entrepreneurial impulse, to seek out opportunity. The game provides us with opportunities in abundance. There is no such thing as a lack of opportunity. There is only a lack of intention and preparation.

As players, we have to understand that opportunities are about collaboration and teamwork. How we communicate ideas inspires and motivates people to create them. Opportunities are most attracted to those looking for them, those who invite them, and those who have the know-how to take advantage of them.

Leadership requires confidence. Confidence walks hand in hand with capability. It is the understanding that we are responsible for delivering on the promises we make.

Capability requires accountability. Accountability is only ever apparent when one takes ownership of his or her nature without leaning on systems of fear that deflect liability. Accepting liability promotes trust. Trust requires love, and love is only ever exchanged through empathy; objective reason outside of fear.

Confidence is a human power that comes from nature. Nature is the only power that exceeds the boundaries of the human form. Humans overwhelmed by their subjective desires cannot understand this because their possessions marginalise them. They can only ever exist in awe of it. The power of confidence makes us desirable and influential amongst players. It is our ability to shape perception.

We must take the time and seek to know ourselves better. We must first seek to understand the derivatives of our own emotionality, and then we must seek to understand them in others.

In a universal economy of ideas, that is, where money exchange is synonymous with meaning, understanding human desire requires we seek deeper insights into our humanity. Consciousness is an understanding that we have a responsibility to the nature of the world rather than catering to the spoils of its nurture.

As an entrepreneur, it is my vision to see this generation and future generations of players win and consciously overcome the man-made rules, which seemingly only serve to benefit the men who made them. The future belongs to us. Tomorrow will reflect the people we choose to be today.

Player, as Aristotle Onassis said, "The rules are ... There are no rules!" Success is a shift in perspective. You either produce or consume. Create or be created. Play or be played. Nothing exists. You choose!

Welcome to the game, entrepreneur!

# REFERENCES

1   Certeau, Michel de. *Heterologies: Discourse on the Other.* Translated by Brian Masumi (Minneapolis: University of Minnesota Press, 1986), 193.

2   Jill Bolte Taylor, "The Neuroanatomical Transformation of the Teenage Brain," TEDxYouth, Indianapolis.

3   G. Danaher, T. Schirato, and J. Webb, *Understanding Foucault* (Australia: Allan & Unwin, 2000), 37–40.

4   Dicks, D.R, *Early Greek Astronomy to Aristotle* (Ithaca, New York: Cornell University Press, 1970), 68.

5   Plato. *The Apology, Phædo and Crito,* trans. by Benjamin Jowett. Vol. II, Part 1. The Harvard Classics (New York: P.F. Collier & Son, 1909–14)

6   "Roy Morgan Market Research: Values-Segments," www.roymorgan.com/products/values-segments.

7   Dale Carnegie, *How to Win Friends and Influence People* (1936; reprint, New York: Simon and Schuster, 1981), 48.

8     Foundation for *A Course in Miracles*, Combined Volume, 3rd ed. (Foundation for Inner Peace, 2007).

9     Walter Isaacson, *Steve Jobs* (New York: Simon & Schuster, 2011)

10    Paul Redding, "Georg Wilhelm Friedrich Hegel," in *The Stanford Encyclopedia of Philosophy* (Spring 2014 Edition), ed. Edward N. Zalta, http://plato.stanford.edu/archives/spr2014/entries/hegel.

11    Peter Singer, "Hegel," in *The Oxford Companion to Philosophy*, ed. T. Honderich (New York: Oxford University Press, 1995).

12    Dale Carnegie, *How to Win Friends and Influence People* (1936; reprint, New York: Simon and Schuster, 1981), 48.

13    Warrillow, John 2010, *Built to Sell: Creating a Business that can Thrive Without You*, Penguin Group, New York, p. 23.

14    John Warrillow, *Built to Sell: Creating a Business that can Thrive Without You* (New York: Penguin Group, 2010), 23.

15    Dale Carnegie, *How to Win Friends and Influence People* (1936; reprint, New York: Simon and Schuster, 1981), 48.

16    Ibid., 94.

17    W. R. Langbauer Jr., K. Payne, R. Charif, E. Rappaport, and F. Osborn, "African elephants respond to distant playbacks of low-frequency conspecific calls," *Journal of Experimental Biology* 157 (1991): 35–46.

18    Ibid.

19    Jaak Panksepp, *Affective Neuroscience: The Foundations of Human and Animal Emotions* (New York: Oxford University Press, 1998), 240.

20    Aristotle, *Aristotle's Metaphysics* (Grinnell, Iowa: The Peripatetic Press,1966)

21    Hugh Benson, *Socratic Wisdom: The Model of Knowledge in Plato's Early Dialogues* (New York: Oxford University Press, 2000)

# FURTHER READINGS

*Folie et deraison: histoire de la folie à l'âge classique*, English ed. 1961.

Howard, Richard, trans. *Madness and Civilization: A History of Insanity in the Age of Reason*. London: Tavistock, 1982.

*Surveiller et punir: naissance de la prison*, English ed. 1975.

Sheridan, Alan, trans. *Discipline and Punish: The Birth of the Prison*. New York: Vintage, 1995.

Wallas, Graham. *The Art of Thought*. London: Jonathan Cape, 1926.

Dostoyevsky, Fyodor. *Crime and Punishment*. London: Penguin Group, 2003.

Kojeve, Alexandre. *Introduction to the Reading of Hegel*. Edited by Allan Bloom. Translated by James Nichols. Ithaca: Cornell University Press, 1986.

Kahn, Thomas 1970, *The Structure of Scientific Revolutions*, University of Chicago Press, Chicago

Merleau-Ponty, Maurice. *Phenomenology of Perception*. Translated by Colin Smith. London: Routledge, 1992.

Ransom, John. *Foucault's Discipline: The Politics of Subjectivity*. Durham and London: Duke University Press, 1997.

Danaher, G., T. Schirato, and J. Webb. *Understanding Foucault*. Australia: Allan & Unwin, 2000.

Waal, Fans de. *The Age of Empathy: Nature's Lessons for a Kinder Society*. London: Souvenir Press, 2010.

Carnegie, Dale. *How to Win Friends and Influence People*. 1936. Reprint, New York: Simon and Schuster, 1981.

Ury, William. *Getting Past No: Negotiating with Difficult People*. London: Random House, 1991.

Cialdini, Robert B. *Influence: The Psychology of Persuasion*. New York: HarperCollins, 2007.

Warrillow, John. *Built to Sell: Creating a Business that can Thrive Without You*. New York: Penguin Group, 2010.

Panksepp, Jaak. *Affective Neuroscience: The Foundations of Human and Animal Emotions*. New York: Oxford University Press, 1998.

Foundation for *A Course in Miracles*, combined volume, 3rd ed. Foundation for Inner Peace, 2007.

McAuslan, Ian. *Greece & Rome*, 2nd series. United Kingdom: Cambridge University Press, 2003.

Pippin, Robert B. *Hegel's Idealism: The Satisfactions of Self-Consciousness*. Cambridge: Cambridge University Press, 1989.

Redding, Paul. "Georg Wilhelm Friedrich Hegel." In *The Stanford Encyclopedia of Philosophy* (Spring 2014 ed.), ed. Edward N. Zalta, http://plato.stanford.edu/archives/spr2014/entries/hegel.